GRACE
Stories

BOB GEORGE

HARVEST HOUSE PUBLISHERS
Eugene, Oregon 97402

Cover by Terry Dugan Design, Minneapolis, Minnesota

GRACE STORIES
Copyright © 2000 by Bob George
Published by Harvest House Publishers
Eugene, Oregon 97402

Library of Congress Cataloging-in-Publication Data

George, Bob, 1933–
    Grace stories / Bob George.
        p. cm.
    ISBN 0-7369-0264-3
    1. Christian life. I. Title.
BV4501.2.G423 2000
242—dc21   99-089970

Contents

Word Pictures of Grace

The Puzzle Comes Together

Word Pictures
of Grace

W<small>HEN</small> J<small>ESUS</small> C<small>HRIST</small> WALKED THIS EARTH, He healed the sick, He fed the multitudes, He performed miracles, and as the apostle John says, He "did many other things as well. If every one of them were written down, I suppose that even the whole world would not have room for the books that would be written" (John 21:25).

But of all the things that Jesus did, one of the most frequent was to teach. Mark 10:1 tells us that when the crowds came to Him, "as was his custom, he taught them."

In fact, Jesus was, and is, the greatest teacher who has ever lived. Those who heard Him said that He taught with great authority. Anyone with a teachable heart, from the youngest person to the oldest, could understand the depths of His message.

This was in part because of the *way* Jesus taught. Mark 4:2 records "he taught them many things by parables." Jesus loved to use physical illustrations and parables to reveal spiritual truth. For example, He used the illustration of a grapevine and its branches to show us our need to live in dependency on Him. He described the different types of soil to teach us about a person's heart—how it responds to the gospel and which type of soil will produce fruit. In the parable of the prodigal son, He used the story of a repentant, wayward son to give us a picture of what the Father love of God is like.

For those who heard Jesus in person and for us today who read the Word of God, these word pictures help plant spiritual truth deep in our hearts. And if we watch carefully what goes on around us, we'll often see examples in our own lives that illustrate God's love and grace. That's how I've learned most of what I know today about my personal relationship with Jesus Christ.

Throughout my 30 years as His child, God has embedded the truths of His Word in my heart by showing me illustrations either in nature or through life's circumstances. These illustrations became so helpful in my own spiritual growth that I began using them to teach other people as well. As a result of my teaching this way for many years in seminars, books, and on my radio broadcast, *People to People,* we frequently receive letters at our Dallas ministry headquarters from people who tell us that a particular illustration I've used has made God's grace clear to them.

Because of the impact these stories have had, Harvest House has asked to publish many of my favorite illustrations—"grace stories" as we're calling them—in book form, with the hope that even more Christians will be able to clearly grasp some of the Bible's most important lessons.

I've discovered that grace stories can also be effective tools to help you understand the depths of God's love and grace and to help explain the gospel to others. Each story stands by itself and explains one aspect of the gospel.

I've placed the stories in an order that progressively explains the fullness of the gospel. The book begins with stories that point out the deity of Christ and the reliability of the Word of God and ends with those that explain the freedom that we have in Him. Along the way are stories that illustrate the vital concepts of forgiveness, life, the believer's identity in Christ, law and grace, dependency, and truth.

The number one question that I'm asked is, "How can I effectively teach the grace of God to my children?" *Grace Stories* is a great place to start. The simplicity of the stories makes them ideal for conveying the simplicity of the gospel to children.

Through the years Christians of all ages have benefited from the 59 stories that follow. It's my prayer that God will use *Grace Stories* to reach an even greater number of Christians with the wonderful message of our freedom in Christ.

Part One

JESUS Christ

Chapter 1

Liar, Lunatic, or Lord?

When Jesus came to the region of Caesarea Philippi, he asked his disciples, "Who do people say the Son of Man is?" They replied, "Some say John the Baptist; others say Elijah; and still others, Jeremiah or one of the prophets." "But what about you?" he asked. "Who do you say I am?"

Matthew 16:13-15

IF YOU WERE TO VISIT ANYWHERE in the world today, talk to people of any religion, and ask, "Who, in your opinion, is the most outstanding personality of all time?" you would most likely get the answer "Jesus of Nazareth."

No matter how devout people may be or how committed to their particular religion, if they consider the facts, they will have to acknowledge that there has never been a man like Jesus of Nazareth. He is the unique personality of all time.

He is the One who has changed the whole course of history—so much so that someone once described history as "His story." Remove Jesus of Nazareth from history, and the past 2000 years would be drastically different.

But who is this Jesus of Nazareth? Is He a great moral teacher as some claim? Or is He a great religious leader like Buddha or Muhammad? Or is He a prophet like the prophets of the Old Testament?

These are some of the answers people have given about Christ's identity. But are these reasonable conclusions, based on what Christ claimed concerning His identity?

Upon examining Christ's claims, C.S. Lewis observed in the book *Mere Christianity:*

> A man who was merely a man and said the sort of things Jesus said would not be a great moral teacher. He would either be a lunatic—on a level with the man who says he is a poached egg—or else he would be the Devil of Hell. You must make your choice. Either this man was, and is, the Son of God: or else a madman or something worse. You can shut him up for a fool; or you can spit at Him and kill Him as a demon; or you can fall at His feet and call him Lord and God. But let us not come up with any patronizing nonsense about His being a great moral teacher. He has not left that open to us. He did not intend to.

Christ's claims were so outrageous that they leave us with only three options. Jesus was either a liar, or He was a lunatic, or He was the Son of the living God.

By His own words, Christ claimed to be the latter. Throughout the Gospels He said things such as, "I and the Father are one" (John 10:30), and "Don't you know me, Philip, even after I have been among you such a long time? Anyone who has seen me has seen the Father" (John 14:9). He made many other statements concerning His divine identity. That His claims to being

God were clearly understood by His hearers is evidenced by their response.

To His statement "I tell you the truth...before Abraham was born, *I am!*" (John 8:58 emphasis added), the Jews "picked up stones to stone him." They knew exactly what Jesus was claiming concerning Himself. They knew only too well the story in the third chapter of Exodus: God met with Moses and appointed him as the one who would lead Israel out of Egypt. Moses asked God what he should answer if the Israelites asked God's name. God said to him, "I AM WHO I AM. This is what you are to say to the Israelites: I AM has sent me to you" (Exodus 3:14). Jesus Christ was thus claiming to be the God of Abraham, Isaac, and Jacob.

Later, these same Pharisees, eager to condemn Jesus, once again attempted to stone Him. When Jesus asked for which miracle they were condemning Him, they replied, "We are not stoning you for any of these...but for blasphemy, because you, a mere man, claim to be God" (John 10:33). And when Jesus told the Pharisees, "My Father is always at his work to this very day, and I, too, am working," the Bible records that the Jews tried all the harder to kill Him, since Jesus wasn't only breaking the Sabbath, "he was even calling God his own Father, making himself equal with God" (John 5:17,18).

The Pharisees knew that Jesus was claiming to be God. Their response makes it clear that they didn't believe these claims. We also know from their response that they didn't conclude that Jesus was a great man, or a good moral teacher, or even a prophet. He was someone they felt they must kill, not because they felt He was a threat to society, but because He was a threat to *them*. Their fears were expressed in John 11:48, "If we let him go on like this, everyone will believe in him, and then the Romans will come and take away both our place and our nation."

Another group of people responded to Jesus in a manner totally different from the Pharisees. The apostles and the writers of the New Testament heard Jesus coming through loud and clear, just as the Pharisees did. Matthew, Luke, Mark, John, Paul, Peter, and the writer of Hebrews all wrote that Jesus was and is God. Unlike the Pharisees, however, these New Testament writers didn't try to kill Jesus. They proclaimed His divinity, and they took His message to the world. As a result, they were ridiculed and mocked, and most of them were killed. To them it was impossible to conclude that Jesus was merely a great man, a moral teacher, or a prophet. Instead, they chose to believe His words, proclaim Him as Lord, and surrender their lives to Him.

No, these men and many others who heard what Jesus claimed concerning Himself didn't conclude that He was a great moral teacher or a prophet. Jesus' claims forced them to conclude that He was either a liar, a lunatic, or God in the flesh. These were the only options available.

Throughout history many people who have read the Gospel accounts of Jesus' life have characterized His identity in all sorts of ways: religious leader, miracle worker, great teacher, perhaps prophet. However, once a person is confronted with Christ's claims, he's forced to decide among the same three options as the Pharisees and the apostles.

Jesus asked His disciples, "But what about you? Who do you say that I am?" His question remains for us to answer today. Who do *you* say that Jesus is?

After examining the facts, are you willing to accept Jesus Christ for who He claimed to be—God? If so, are you willing to give your life to Him? If you do, you'll find in Him everything you've been looking for.

Jesus Christ invites each of us:

Come to me, all you who are weary and burdened, and I will give you rest. Take my yoke upon you and learn from me, for I am gentle and humble in heart, and you will find rest for your souls. For my yoke is easy and my burden is light.

Matthew 11:28-30

Chapter 2

The Hindu and the Anthill

In the beginning was the Word, and the Word was with God, and the Word was God....The Word became flesh and made his dwelling among us. We have seen his glory, the glory of the One and Only, who came from the Father, full of grace and truth.

John 1:1,14

ALTHOUGH I DIDN'T BECOME A CHRISTIAN until I was 36, I grew up believing that Jesus Christ was the Son of God. The problem was, I didn't know what that meant or what importance it held for me personally. However, I believed it so strongly that when one of my fraternity brothers in college denied that Jesus was the Son of God, I punched him out.

Although the Bible teaches that Jesus is God, the question remains: How could God become a man—and why? This is very difficult for us to understand. To many people, the very fact that Jesus Christ came to earth as "one of us" proves that He couldn't be God. Therefore, His death on the cross has little significance. To them, He was simply a good man who died a horrible death.

However, the apostle Paul wrote: "Although He existed in the form of God, [He] did not regard equality with God a thing to be grasped, but emptied Himself, taking the form of a bond-servant, and being made in the likeness of men. And being found in appearance as a man, He humbled Himself by becoming obedient to the point of death, even death on a cross" (Philippians 2:6-8 NASB).

A good illustration of Jesus' incarnation is the story of several Christian college students who shared the gospel with a Hindu classmate. The young man believed in God, yet he couldn't grasp the Christian concept that God actually visited this planet in the person of Jesus Christ and died to take away our sins.

One day while walking through a field and wrestling with this Christian concept of God, he observed an anthill that was in the path of a farmer plowing his field. The particular Hindu sect he belonged to believed that all life was sacred: A cow, a cobra, even an ant was of inestimable value.

Gripped with a concern similar to what you or I would feel for hundreds of people trapped inside a burning building, the Hindu wanted to warn the ants of the impending danger. But how? He could shout to them, but they wouldn't hear. He could write to them, but they wouldn't be able to read.

How then could he communicate with the ants?

Then it struck him. Out of sheer love, he wished that he could become an ant. If this were possible, he could warn them before it was too late. Then he realized this was what his Christian classmates had been trying to tell him about Jesus.

At last he understood how God had called to us, but we wouldn't listen. He wrote to us, but we refused to read. Out of sheer love, Jesus Christ—God Himself—stepped out of heaven and took on a body of human flesh. He became like us and lived a perfect life. He led us away from the death and destruction looming over us by becoming a sin-offering in our place. He demonstrated His love for us on a cross because it's through His death on that cross that we escape the penalty for our sins.

Why did God become man? He did so to save us from our sins and to give us His very life.

Have you settled in your own mind the truth of Christ's perfect humanity and complete deity? Are you willing to trust in what He did for you as your only source of salvation? As the apostle Paul said in Romans 5:8—

God demonstrates his own love for us in this: While we were still sinners, Christ died for us.

Chapter 3

The Sheepdog and the Shepherd

Now while he was in Jerusalem at the Passover Feast, many people saw the miraculous signs he was doing and believed in his name. But Jesus would not entrust himself to them, for he knew all men. He did not need man's testimony about man, for he knew what was in a man.

John 2:23-25

T HERAPY SEEMS TO BE THE ANSWER for everything these days. Psychologists, psychiatrists, or psychoanalysts—the so-called experts of the day—appear on TV and radio talk shows daily, giving Americans the "answers" to all their problems.

Our nation seems to have gone counseling-crazy. It's almost a status symbol to have a therapist. Even Christians aren't excluded from this counseling mania. What appears on Christian TV and radio isn't much different than secular network programming. We simply dress up worldly solutions in a Christian suit and proclaim them as God's answer to our problems.

In light of this counseling craze, what role should Christian counselors play in the lives of believers? The answer was made evident to me one night when my wife, Amy, received a phone call from a friend. This woman needed counsel for a particular situation in her life, and so Amy talked with her several hours, explaining that Christ was the answer to her problem.

At the end of the conversation, this friend wondered about coming to our People to People ministry headquarters for more counseling and asked if Amy thought she needed to.

"Yes," Amy answered, "because the counselors are like a *bunch of sheepdogs herding the sheep back to the shepherd.*"

This is the best illustration I've ever heard describing the role of Christian counselors. We don't have the answers to life's problems. But as Christians, we know Someone who does. And our role, like that of a sheepdog, is to make sure the sheep make it safely back to the Shepherd.

This role is important for several reasons.

First, Jesus Christ created each of us. "By him all things were created: things in heaven and on earth, visible and invisible, whether thrones or powers or rulers or authorities; all things were created by him and for him" (Colossians 1:16).

Because Jesus Christ created us, He *knows* us. He knows what makes us tick, what our needs are, and what's best for us in this life. No one else could possibly know as much about people as the One who created them.

Somehow many Christians have forgotten that they were created by Jesus Christ. Instead, they've fallen prey to the latest insights of the psychological community. For some reason, they've bought the idea that Freud, Jung, Skinner, or Rogers knows more about man than Jesus does.

The apostle Paul made a universal statement about our insight into man's behavior: "I do not understand what I do" (Romans 7:15).

Freud doesn't understand why people do what they do. Neither does Jung, Skinner, Rogers, or anyone else. The only One who knows the truth about people is Jesus Christ. He's the only One who understands why we do what we do: "Many people... believed in his name. But Jesus would not entrust himself to them, for he knew all men. He did not need man's testimony about man, for he knew what was in a man" (John 2:23-25).

Second, Jesus Christ loves us. "God so loved the world that he gave his one and only Son, that whoever believes in him shall not perish but have eternal life" (John 3:16).

Someone once remarked to me about his psychiatrist, "Once the money stopped, so did the love and compassion." Jesus Christ is the only One who can love and accept us as we are, and who does so *freely*.

Such love is hard for us to believe. In our minds we think that God must be our enemy. We try to do good, but we continue to sin and fall flat on our face.

God, however, not only says that He loves us, but He also showed us that love through His Son, Jesus Christ. "God demonstrates his own love for us in this: While we were still sinners, Christ died for us" (Romans 5:8).

And finally, Jesus Christ claims to be the solution to every need of the human heart. To the hunger and craving in the depth of our soul, Jesus answers, "*I am!*"

He's our bread of life, the light of the world. He's the way, the truth, and the life; the Alpha and the Omega. He's the resurrection and the life. He's the good shepherd who laid down His life for His sheep; and now, resurrected from the dead, He cares for His sheep.

If we're to find the answers to our problems, we *must* turn to Him.

Are you looking for answers in life?

Jesus said, "Come to me."

In Him you'll find rest for your soul, because in Him you will find everything you need to experience the abundant life here on earth.

Are you trying to help other people with their problems? If so, be a good sheepdog. Recognize that your role is to point people back to the Shepherd.

Chapter 4

Plane Faith

*B*ut the righteous man shall live by faith.

Romans 1:17 NASB

LIVING BY FAITH IS A LIFE OF OBJECTIVITY. It's either valid or foolish based on its *object*. I like to compare faith to swallowing. Someone might say, "Swallowing enables you to live," and that sounds right. Swallowing food *does* enable me to live.

However, I could also swallow *poison* and *die*, using the same mechanism that I use to swallow food to live. So it isn't the *swallowing itself* that nourishes me; it's the *object* of my swallowing—food—that gives strength to my body.

Another good example that shows the importance of faith's object is flying in an airplane.

Let's say you're leaving on a vacation and you have a ticket for passage on a major airline. Is it reasonable to take the flight? The facts tell us that flying is an extremely safe way to travel. Only a bare fraction of one percent of flights crash. In fact, traveling long distances by air is safer than driving the same distances.

Even so, we must admit that there's a certain leap of faith involved, because you have to take 100 percent of yourself on the plane. But is it *reasonable*?

Even though your emotions may be a little jumpy about flying, based on the *facts* you would be making a reasonable decision of faith by entrusting yourself to the jet to take you to your destination. Few people would call that decision one of "blind faith" or an "irrational leap."

However, suppose I call you to come over and look at a tremendous new invention of mine. I take you into my backyard and proudly show you the "airplane" I've just built. There it is—a contraption made out of plywood, wires, old tires, and a lawnmower engine. Then I explain my plan to take it up for a test flight.

I want to get a good running start off the side of a cliff, and I invite you to go along. When you hesitate, I ask with an offended tone, "What's the matter? Don't you trust me?"

Your only honest and intelligent answer would be, "*No*, I don't trust you!"

Suppose I respond: "Your problem is that you don't have enough faith! You're a negative thinker. If you have enough faith, it will work."

Listen, it doesn't matter how much faith you or I have; if we go off a cliff in my homemade airplane, we'll both hit bottom together.

You can see from these two illustrations—swallowing poison and the rickety Bob George airplane—that the *amount* of faith isn't the issue. The issue is *the trustworthiness of the object.* A person could get on a 727 with fear and trembling but find himself landing safe and sound a few hours later. Another person could get in my homemade flying machine with absolute confidence and total faith and yet come down like a rock as soon as we left the cliff.

The *object*, not the *amount* of faith is the issue.

So it is in our Christian life. The Bible tells us that the righteous will live by faith. But faith in what?

For Christians, the object of our faith is *Christ Himself.* He's the one to whom we totally commit our being, our safety, and our security.

*H*e who believes in Him shall not be disappointed.

1 Peter 2:6 NASB

Part Two

THE WORD OF God

Chapter 5

Admiral Byrd

You diligently study the Scriptures because you think that by them you possess eternal life. These are the Scriptures that testify about me, yet you refuse to come to me to have life....

John 5:39,40

No DOUBT YOU'VE HEARD THIS STATEMENT: "Everything is relative; there are no absolutes." Of course the speaker is *absolutely* sure of that! The sad fact is that a person who has bought into the lie that there are no absolutes will, sooner or later, exhibit the sad results of this belief.

Most of us know there *are* absolutes. We were created to need something sure on which to lay a firm foundation to help us maintain stability throughout our lives. But until we come to understand this truth, our lives will remain unstable in all ways.

In the world of science, all experimentation starts from the premise of a "constant"—something sure, unmoving, unchanging—in order to arrive at consistently accurate conclusions. Without this constant, the researcher can never be sure of his findings.

A dramatic example of this need for a constant is the story of Admiral Richard Byrd's first Antarctic expedition.

Admiral Byrd flew to the frigid South Pole and there spent the six-month-long night alone. Snow after snow and blast after blast buried his small hut.

Each day he shoveled his way to the surface in order to get some exercise. There was only enough light to see a dozen yards or so as he walked the few steps he dared take.

On one such outing, having ventured as far as he thought wise, he turned to discover with shock that he couldn't see the stovepipe of his hut. Veteran that he was, the admiral controlled his tendency to panic, refusing to move because he knew that to wander about without direction could take him farther from the hut.

Byrd calmly drove a stake into the snow, tied a rope to it and, using the stake as his center or constant, walked a large circle around it. Not finding his hut, he let out the rope a bit, extending his radius, and walked another circle, searching through the blackness while keeping the stake in sight. The third time he tried, the circle was so large that he almost lost sight of the stake. He returned to it—his constant—and resolved to make one more attempt, with a still larger circle.

The range of visibility was very small as he walked, holding visually to the stake—his point of reference. He knew if he lost sight of the stake the ice and snow would quickly claim another victim. It was then that he walked squarely into the tunnel of his hut.

Byrd had relied on something sure and unchanging. And though he had groped through icy darkness, he never lost sight of his constant as it guided him to shelter and security.

Another example of a constant is the carpenter's use of a plumb line when erecting a tall building. Without a plumb line, a builder will create a new Leaning Tower of Pisa.

At home, have you ever tried to hang wallpaper without a plumb line? What a mess!

So too, we must build our lives to a plumb line, or a constant, that's reliable and neverchanging. Nowadays humanism tells us that everything is relative. That's a modern way of saying that happy lives can be built without plumb lines. When it comes to the things of God, relativism is sheer idiocy.

We are the most blessed people on earth to have the Bible as our plumb line. What a privilege to order our lives around His neverchanging Word—which Jesus Himself affirmed in John 17:17 when He declared, "Your word is truth."

Like a skilled carpenter, we too must have a plumb line. Like Admiral Byrd we too must drive a stake. If we choose to live without such a constant upon which to rest our beliefs and base our judgments, we wander aimlessly, groping about in darkness—lost.

We are human variables, walking about: happy one moment, sad the next. There's nothing constant in our life—unless as a Christian we have driven a stake by placing our security in Jesus Christ, the living Word. For He is the only constant of which we can say, "[He] is the same yesterday, today and forever" (Hebrews 13:8).

Some people have trouble reading the Bible. They get lost, or their mind wanders. But it's not enough just to read the Word—we must know the living Word, Jesus Christ. The Pharisees of Jesus' day knew what the Scriptures said but didn't have a clue as to what they meant. Christ is our constant—He gives us the ability to see what God's Word is saying to us.

The Bible provides a plumb line, a point of reference, a stake around which we must move in order to maintain stability in our lives. Whatever situation we find ourselves in, we can bounce our questions and concerns off the unchanging truth of God's Word.

The lesson from Admiral Byrd holds an important secret: to keep our eyes on Christ—our constant—as we explore more of our exciting and adventurous life in Him.

Chapter 6

Billy Graham's Life-Changing Decision

They received the word with great eagerness, examining the Scriptures daily, to see whether these things were so.

Acts 17:11 NASB

THE BIBLE IS MANY THINGS at the same time. It's the autobiography of God, a study in human behavior, a historical account, a counselor's manual, a textbook on life, a telescope looking into the future, a storehouse of riches, and a love letter.

It's a library of answers given to us out of the heart of a loving God. It describes all the riches and treasures He has given to us, His children. The Word of God can fill every human need, and that's why it's important for us to learn how to use this unique book.

Every child of God must individually come to grips with the authority of the Bible, as Billy Graham did early in his ministry. Through the influence of a close friend who harbored serious doubts about the integrity of the Scriptures, and through extensive reading of other people's opinions on theological questions, Mr. Graham found himself growing more and more confused in his own view of the Bible.

Was the Bible still to be accepted as an infallible standard, even in the face of problems too hard to resolve? Could he continue to trust a gospel message which came from a book questioned by many intelligent, educated men? These questions plagued Mr. Graham for a long time.

Finally in the summer of 1949, while attending a conference in Forest Home, California, Mr. Graham had a final confrontation with God about the trustworthiness of the Bible. Author John Pollock recorded it in *Billy Graham: The Authorized Biography*:

> [Mr. Graham] saw that intellect alone could not resolve the question of authority. He must go beyond intellect. He thought of the faith he used constantly in daily life: he did not know how a train or a plane or a car worked, but he rode them. He did not know why a brown cow could eat green grass and yield white milk, but he drank milk. Was it only in the things of the Spirit that the exercising of faith was wrong?

> "So I went back and I got my Bible," Graham recalled, "and I went out in the moonlight. And I got to a stump and put the Bible on the stump and I knelt down and said, 'O God, I cannot prove certain things. I cannot answer some of the questions...people are raising, but I accept this Book by faith as the Word of God.'"

The incident was immediately followed by the largest evangelistic campaign of Billy Graham's entire ministry, one that launched him into a worldwide ministry.

Have you ever, like Billy Graham, personally accepted by faith the entire Bible as the Word of God?

If not, why not do so now?

Here is a suggested prayer:

Father, thank You for leaving Your holy Word with us. Thank You for giving me Your Spirit so I can understand Your very mind as revealed in Your Word. Beginning today I accept by faith the authority of Your Word over my life, and I trust it without reserve as Your personal Word to me.

Chapter 7

Jonah and the Whale

Sanctify them by the truth; your word is truth.

John 17:17

HAVE YOU EVER HEARD PEOPLE SAY they can't believe the Bible because it contains stories such as Jonah's being swallowed by a big fish, or Noah's building an ark to survive the flood, or even the account of creation?

"Come on!" they say. "How do you expect me to believe the Bible when it contains so many fairy tales?"

But are these stories merely fairy tales, or did they really happen? And how can we know for sure?

Trying to prove to a skeptic that Jonah was actually swallowed by a fish will get you into an argument that's impossible to win. Even if you could prove that a fish swallowed Jonah, would this be enough to convince a person to give his life to Christ?

In the final analysis, the credibility of the Bible doesn't depend on proving that these stories are true. The validity of the Bible rests on the answer to the question, "Who is Jesus?"

Jesus claimed to be God. If He *is* God, then we can certainly trust what He says about the Word of God. If He is not God, then who cares if Jonah was swallowed by a fish? It won't help you or me get along better in this world today.

Since Jesus Christ *is* God, let's look at what Jesus said concerning Jonah:

> A wicked and adulterous generation asks for a miraculous sign! But none will be given it except the sign of the prophet Jonah. For as Jonah was three days and three nights in the belly of a huge fish, so the Son of Man will be three days and three nights in the heart of the earth. The men of Nineveh will stand up at the judgment with this generation and condemn it; for they repented at the preaching of Jonah, and now one greater than Jonah is here (Matthew 12:39-41).

In this encounter with the Pharisees, Jesus clearly stated that Jonah was in the belly of a huge fish. As a matter of fact, He compared Jonah's time in the belly of the fish to His three days and nights in the grave before He would be raised from the dead.

Now if Jesus is God, and He said that Jonah was in a fish, then Jonah *was* in a fish. I would believe the story if He said *Jonah* swallowed the *fish*. Why? Because the validity of this story rests on the truthfulness of the One who spoke it—Jesus Christ.

The reliability of the Word of God rests on the identity of Jesus Christ. All other questions raised by the skeptics concerning Jonah, Noah, and creation are merely smoke screens.

In all my years of ministry, I've never encountered a person on his deathbed who wondered about Jonah. People in trouble are interested only in finding out if Jesus really is who He claimed to be, and if so, can He solve their problems?

Jesus Christ testified to the Bible's veracity when He said, "Your word is truth." Because *Jesus* stated that God's Word is truth, we can rest confidently in the fact the Bible holds all the answers to life's problems.

The real question we need to ask then is, "Who is Jesus?"

Because Jesus is *God*, we can rest confidently in the fact the Word is truth. We can also know that Jonah was in a fish, that Noah built an ark to survive the flood, and that the world was created in six days through God's spoken word. These events are actual history—not because they can be proven scientifically, but because Jesus said they happened.

Have you settled in your mind the real question, "Who is Jesus?"

If not, do so today. Then you can be assured that God's Word is true. And as Jesus said,

You will know the truth, and the truth will set you free.

John 8:32

Chapter 8

Have a Seat

You believe that there is one God. Good!
Even the demons believe that—and shudder.

James 2:19

If WE KNOW INTELLECTUALLY that the Bible is the Word of God, and we acknowledge with our minds that Jesus Christ is the Son of God, do we have true faith?

The difference between intellectual belief and true faith is explained by a simple illustration I often use in teaching. Standing behind the podium, I point to a chair in the front row and say, "I can honestly tell you that I believe with all my heart that chair will support me if I sit in it. There's not a shadow of doubt in my mind that chair is trustworthy. That's the truth."

But I'm not exercising what the Bible calls faith in that chair. The word "faith" in the Bible includes the elements of dependence and reliance. Regardless of what I think or even what I say, I'm not demonstrating what the Bible calls faith until I park my body down on it.

Now imagine that I hold out a giftwrapped present and say, "Here, this present is for you." You look admiringly at the present. You compliment me on the gift wrap, you may even act excited that I'm giving you a gift. But all the while I remain standing in front of you holding out the present, it's not yet yours. I've offered it, and you've expressed belief that I'm offering it to you; but when does it really become yours? When does your faith in what I am promising about that gift result in your having it?

Just as sitting in the chair will show your faith in its ability to hold you, so too will the gift become yours when you exercise your faith by reaching to my outstretched arms and taking the offered present as your own.

Faith always involves a decision of the will to act on what the mind believes is true. Believing that the chair is capable of supporting me is not the same thing as actually sitting down in it. Thanking me for the present I offer, without actually taking it, is meaningless.

Saying we believe the Word of God without availing ourselves of its riches or living by its wisdom is also meaningless.

Faith always responds to the truth with action.

Chapter 9

Wilbur and the Word of God

The Spirit searches all things, even the deep things of God....No one knows the thoughts of God except the Spirit of God.

1 Corinthians 2:10,12

THE APOSTLE PAUL TELLS US, "Eye has not seen, nor ear heard, nor have entered into the heart of man the things which God has prepared for those who love Him. But God has revealed them to us through His Spirit" (1 Corinthians 2:9,10 NKJV) Anyone, whether lost or saved, can read the Bible and understand the words in it. But what does it mean, and how does it apply to our lives? To know this requires the teaching of the Holy Spirit. Only He can reveal the meaning of God's Word.

To truly understand those things which God has freely given us, we must approach the Word of God with an attitude of dependence on God's Spirit to reveal its meaning.

A humble man named Wilbur, whom I met almost 20 years ago, has stood as a reminder and inspiration to me to continue studying God's Word with this attitude.

I had only been a Christian about a year and was still working in the floor-covering business. I was attending an executive meeting in New York that required a long limousine ride from the airport.

I asked Wilbur, the chauffeur, whether he minded if I rode up front with him. He had no objection, so I got in the front passenger seat and as Wilbur drove, we chatted a while. I found that I liked Wilbur very much and wanted to bring up the issue of Christ.

"Wilbur, have you ever heard the good news about Jesus Christ?" I asked.

Wilbur shot upright in his seat and asked excitedly, "Are you a Christian?"

"Yes," I answered, "are you?"

"Yes, sir!" he said. "Boy, it's great to have a Christian riding with me. I don't get to meet too many folks who know Jesus around here."

The rest of that hour-long ride was sheer pleasure.

The next two days I spent in our board meeting. I learned very quickly why they're called "bored" meetings. At the conclusion, the CEO offered to take me back to the airport. "Oh no," I said, "I don't want to bother you that much. I'll ride with Wilbur."

After all the superficial business hoopla, Wilbur was a huge breath of fresh air. We talked about how we had come to believe in Christ, about how knowing Him had changed our family lives, and of what we had learned about life in general.

As we talked, it became obvious to me that Wilbur was an extremely wise man. Through his years of enjoying an intimate relationship with Christ, the wisdom of God had come to permeate his being. My respect for him grew as the time passed.

Then the conversation took an unexpected turn. As I was talking about my experience of studying the Word of God, Wilbur mentioned that he didn't own a Bible.

"You don't own a Bible?" I asked, very surprised. "Well, I'd like to give you one, Wilbur. Just give me your address, and as soon as I get back to the office I'll mail you one."

Wilbur was hesitant, and he mumbled something with a troubled look on his face. Then he said, "Mr. George, that would be nice of you, but it wouldn't be worth your time or money. I don't know how to read."

I was shocked. Here was a man with as solid a grasp on biblical truth as I had ever encountered, and yet he was saying that he didn't even have the ability to read the Bible.

"Then how have you learned so much, Wilbur?" I asked. His big grin returned.

"I may not be able to read, Mr. George, but *I listen real good!* I love Jesus, and so whenever I get a chance to learn some more about Him in church or on the radio, I perk up my ears and pray that God will teach me. And He always does."

When I got home I sent Wilbur something he *could* use—the New Testament on cassette tapes—and I have little doubt that he has used them to his full advantage.

Regardless of his inability to read, Wilbur has the most important qualities for growing in grace: a heart of love for God, an attitude of humble faith, and a teachable spirit. Most important of all, he has never forgotten that *his first love is a Person.* Upon those foundation stones the Lord Jesus Christ can construct a solid life. All a person with these attitudes needs is access to the truth of God, whether through reading or hearing.

My life was permanently affected by Wilbur's example. His hunger to learn has reminded me to take advantage of the reading ability God has given me. But at the same time, the wisdom Wilbur attained without formal education has reminded me not to become too enamored of my own knowledge. I've learned that if I go to the Bible seeking only knowledge, I'll get knowledge and nothing else. That's a great prescription for spiritual burnout! However, if my desire is to know Christ Himself, He will reveal Himself to me, and teach me whatever knowledge I need at the same time.

The next time you read the Word of God, remember Wilbur and approach the Bible with a humble heart, trusting the Spirit to reveal the truth of God's love and grace.

Chapter 10

Hungry for the Word

I am the bread of life. He who comes to me will never go hungry, and he who believes in me will never be thirsty.

John 6:35

IN SPITE OF THE FACT THAT classic Christianity is full of good news, there's still resistance and objections from many people. This is where we begin to run into the "buts" and "what abouts?" "I know we're under grace, but…", "I know we're totally forgiven, but…", "I know Christ lives in us, but…"

That's when we become what I call "billy-goat Christians": "But—but—but."

We're simply afraid to believe that God really means what He says.

Bible study and prayer are two issues that are brought up repeatedly as examples. Recently a man asked me, "But if you don't keep people under the law, how do you get them to study their Bibles? How do you get them to pray?"

He was honestly bewildered. I knew that his background included a great deal of Bible study and Scripture memorization, but to him these were "disciplines."

His working assumption was that Christians don't want to do these things, and that they need to be firmly pressured to do them.

"Let me ask you a question," I countered. "Did you ever get a letter from someone you were in love with?"

"Yes," he answered.

"And did anyone have to tell you to read it?" I asked.

"No, of course not," he admitted—and he saw my point.

If you're like everyone else I've ever met, you'll read a love letter over and over, backward and forward, and between the lines!

When you're in love, nobody has to tell you to act that way. You just do it. Ever since I was a new Christian, no one has had to tell me to read my Bible. I *want* to do it. I love the Lord, and it's exciting to read His "love letter" to me. Besides, I can't stand the thought of living without the Word, because it's my spiritual food.

Jesus said, "Man does not live on bread alone, but on every word that comes from the mouth of God" (Matthew 4:4).

I read my Bible for the same reason that I eat food—because I'm hungry.

If I were a doctor, and someone came to me and said, "Doc, I have absolutely no appetite for food. I don't mean once in a while; I mean ever," I would immediately know there was something wrong with this person.

Fluctuations in appetite are normal, but absolutely no appetite is a symptom of sickness, and I would try to find out what the cause of it is! And that's exactly the way I respond to a Christian who tells me he has no desire at all to read the Bible or he has no desire to pray or assemble with other believers. That's not normal; that's abnormal.

It's a sign of bondage brought about by error. So I would try to identify the error and replace it with truth from the Word of God.

Just like my physical appetite, my spiritual appetite waxes and wanes. It isn't perfectly consistent, and I don't worry about it if the fluctuations aren't extreme. But there are times, physically, when I get the flu and have no appetite for food at all. Then I'll often have to force myself to eat, knowing that I need to keep my strength up.

In the same way, there are times when I might not have a desire for God's Word, and the reason is because I have started believing the lie of legalism and the accusations of the accuser. At those times, even though I don't have the desire, I'll make myself get into the Bible simply because I know I need to renew my mind with truth. But don't forget, those times are still the abnormal, not the normal state of my spiritual life.

My assumption is when a believer understands the fullness of God's love and acceptance, he'll want to read God's Word; he'll want to spend time with his heavenly Father in prayer; and he'll want to gather with other believers for teaching and encouragement.

It's only natural.

Part
Three

FORGIVENESS

The Dividing Line
of Human History

*For this reason Christ is the mediator of a
new covenant, that those who are called may
receive the promised eternal inheritance—
now that he has died as a ransom to set them
free from the sins committed under the first
covenant. In the case of a will, it is necessary
to prove the death of the one who made it,
because a will is in force only when somebody
has died; it never takes effect while the one
who made it is living.*

Hebrews 9:15-17

IT'S FASCINATING TO ME THAT the birth of Christ is the single
event that divides human history into two parts. Even though
only a small percentage of the world believes that Jesus Christ
is God and the Savior of the world, the world's calendars use
Christ's birth to divide history into B.C. and A.D., with B.C.
meaning "before Christ" and A.D. meaning "in the year of our
Lord." Even though the world doesn't recognize Christ for who
He is, it does recognize that all of human history centers around
Jesus Christ.

God also points to Jesus Christ as the centerpiece of human history. However, while we point to His *birth* as the dividing line, God looks at the *cross* of Jesus Christ as the dividing line of human history. Why? Because Jesus' death on the cross ushered in a brand new covenant. This gives new meaning to our "B.C." and "A.D."

From God's vantage point, B.C. means "before the cross," and as I jokingly say, A.D. means "after de cross." The new covenant had been prophesied throughout the Old Testament, and the day Christ died it went into effect. It's this new covenant that we live under today.

A covenant is the same as a will. For a will or covenant to go into effect, the one who made it must die. Most of us understand this from our legal system. If you have a will, it won't take effect until you die. This is what Hebrews 9:16,17 tells us: "In the case of a will, it is necessary to prove the death of the one who made it, because a will is in force only when somebody has died; it never takes effect while the one who made it is living."

Therefore, for God's promised new covenant to go into effect, Christ had to die.

Now this new covenant is different than the one that God established with the nation of Israel through Moses at Mount Sinai. The old covenant was described by Paul as the "ministry that condemns men" and the "ministry that brought death" (2 Corinthians 3). It was a covenant that required people to live up to its righteous standards. To those who failed it said, "The wages of sin is death" (Romans 6:23). Because people couldn't live up to the requirements of the old covenant, they experienced fear and guilt, and as a result could never draw near to God.

This is why God ushered in a brand new covenant. Hebrews 8:7,8 says, "If there had been nothing wrong with that first covenant, no place would have been sought for another. But God found fault with the people."

The problem with the old covenant was us. That's why God brought in a new covenant, one not dependent on our ability to live up to the law, but totally dependent upon Jesus Christ.

Under the old covenant, the blood of bulls and goats merely covered sins. Under the new covenant, Christ's sacrifice *took away* our sins. Under the old covenant, sacrifices were offered again and again. Under the new covenant, Jesus died for sins *once for all*, and "where these have been forgiven, there is no longer any sacrifice for sin" (Hebrews 10:18).

Under the old covenant, the sacrifices, repeated endlessly year after year, were an annual reminder of sins. Under the new covenant, God remembers our sins and lawless acts no more. Under the old covenant, the wages of sin is death. Under the new covenant, the gift of God is eternal life. Under the old covenant, it was impossible for man to draw near to God. Under the new covenant, we are encouraged to go boldly to the throne of grace calling God "Abba, Father."

Because of the cross, we're no longer under the old covenant. Today we live under the new covenant based on the love and grace of God. Therefore, our acceptance before God is no longer dependent on our self-efforts but on Christ. This is the truth that sets us free.

Are you still relating to God based on the old covenant? Or have you recognized that the cross is the dividing line of human history and as a result of Christ's death on the cross, we live under a brand new covenant?

Because we're under a new covenant, we have a new relationship with God our Father, and we're free to grow in love with Him and enjoy the abundant life that God has provided in the resurrected life of Jesus Christ.

Chapter 12

Accounts Receivable, Accounts Payable

All this is from God, who reconciled us to himself through Christ and gave us the ministry of reconciliation: that God was reconciling the world to himself in Christ, not counting men's sins against them. And he has committed to us the message of reconciliation. We are therefore Christ's ambassadors, as though God were making his appeal through us. We implore you on Christ's behalf: Be reconciled to God.

2 Corinthians 5:18-20

DO YOU FIND THAT MANY CHRISTIANS aren't enjoying their relationship with God? Do you hear: "I know that I'm saved, but I don't feel like God likes me or accepts me," or "I'm sure He's disappointed in me"?

What do you say to someone who thinks he can't approach God with confidence?

The answer is found in the biblical truth of reconciliation. To reconcile means "to settle or resolve." Reconciliation is what

God has done on our behalf regarding the sin issue. He settled it once for all so that we could enjoy a relationship with Him.

One of the best illustrations I know to help explain reconciliation comes from the use of the word in accounting.

Let's say that you sold a piece of merchandise to a customer on credit. Thirty days pass and he fails to make a payment. Sixty days and then 90 days pass, and still no payment. Several months later you discover that the customer is bankrupt and can never pay his bill. At that point the only thing you can do is write off the debt. In other words, you *reconcile* the books by removing the uncollectible debt from your ledger.

By writing the debt off your accounts receivable, you in essence paid a debt that you did not owe for a customer who owed a debt that he could not pay. This is a perfect picture of what Christ's death accomplished for us.

We too owed a debt that we couldn't pay. The Bible declares "all have sinned and fall short of the glory of God" (Romans 3:23). It also declares "the wages of sin is death" (Romans 6:23). Death is the debt we owe. That's what was on God's accounts receivable ledger.

God, however, reconciled His books, and in so doing reconciled us to Himself. Through Christ's death on the cross, God paid a debt that He did not owe: "All this is from God, who reconciled us to himself through Christ and gave us the ministry of reconciliation: that God was reconciling the world to himself in Christ, not counting men's sins against them" (2 Corinthians 5:18,19).

God has reconciled us to Himself and doesn't count our sins against us because Jesus Christ has paid our debt in full at the cross.

> For Christ died for sins once for all, the righteous for
> the unrighteous, to bring you to God (1 Peter 3:18).

> He forgave us all our sins, having canceled the written
> code, with its regulations, that was against us and that
> stood opposed to us; he took it away, nailing it to the
> cross (Colossians 2:13,14).

> This is love: not that we loved God, but that he loved us
> and sent his Son as the one who would turn aside
> [God's] wrath, taking away our sins (1 John 4:10).

These verses show that Jesus Christ has paid the debt for our sins.

Even so, we still tend to see ourselves as God's enemies. Paul writes the Colossians: "Once you were alienated from God and were enemies in your minds because of your evil behavior" (Colossians 1:21).

When we sin, it's so easy to think that God is disappointed or that He will have to punish us. This is only in our minds, however, and doesn't take into account the fact that the punishment due us was taken for us by Jesus Christ.

We may *think* or *feel* that we're God's enemies, but that's not true. God no longer counts our sins against us. As a matter of fact, Hebrews 10:17 states that God no longer *remembers* our sins and lawless acts. God has completely written off our debt. All God sees when He looks at His accounts receivable ledger are the words "Paid in Full!" And when He looks at us, He sees us as holy and perfect.

> Now he has reconciled you by Christ's physical body
> through death to present you holy in his sight, without
> blemish and free from accusation (Colossians 1:22).

> By one sacrifice he has made perfect forever those who
> are being made holy (Hebrews 10:14).

To further help us see that our reconciliation to Him is complete, God tells us: "There is now no condemnation for those who are in Christ Jesus, because through Christ Jesus the law of the Spirit of life set me free from the law of sin and death" (Romans 8:1,2).

God desires to be our friend. He paid our debt in full and removed the sin barrier that stood between us so that we could have a relationship with Him and experience the abundant life He promised. To do so, we must write the debt we owe God off our accounts payable ledger. In other words, we must believe that Christ has done it all. That's *our* role: to rest in the finished work of Christ. That's why Paul writes in 2 Corinthians 5:20, "We implore you on Christ's behalf: Be reconciled to God."

There's nothing left for man to do except believe—believe that God is no longer counting your sins against you, believe that God no longer remembers your sins, believe that you have been forgiven of all sins, believe that God sees you as holy and perfect, believe that there is no more condemnation for those in Christ Jesus.

Are you willing to trust Christ, and Him alone, for your own reconciliation to God? Are you willing to receive the message of God's total love, grace, and forgiveness? Are you willing to accept the plea of God to be reconciled to Him by taking the debt you owe off your accounts payable?

Chapter 13

The Gift in a Gift

In him we have redemption through his blood, the forgiveness of sins, in accordance with the riches of God's grace.

Ephesians 1:7

MOST CHRISTIANS WOULD AGREE THAT Christ lives in them. However, when they are asked, "Do you believe you have total forgiveness of all your sins?" many questions arise. This is because the forgiveness of sins has often been presented to people as a separate offer.

Too many times the gospel presentation has been, "Come down the aisle and receive the forgiveness of sins." Certainly this is part of the good news, but it's not all of the good news.

Salvation isn't like a vending machine, where I put my coin in and get a little forgiveness here, a little holiness there, or a little power of some sort. The gospel message is an invitation to turn to the person of Jesus Christ by faith. And when you have received *Him*, you have received *everything*.

To get a better understanding of this, let's say I hold a pen in one hand and a Bible in the other. Let the pen represent forgiveness and the Bible represent Christ. I then place the pen within the open pages and close the Bible. Where's the pen? Obviously, it's in the Bible. Now if the pen represents forgiveness and the Bible represents Christ, where is forgiveness found? It's found in Christ. It's impossible to have one without the other. If I were to hand you the Bible, you would have the pen as well. But you might say, "All I want is the pen." But you can't have the pen apart from the book. It is a two-for-one deal.

So it is with forgiveness. The issue in salvation is Christ Himself—not what He can do for you, but His offering His very life to you. The moment you receive Christ, you receive His total forgiveness *because forgiveness is in Him.*

That's why Ephesians 1:7 says, "In him we have…forgiveness of sins." All that God has to offer us is in His Son, Jesus Christ.

To believe that Christ lives in you and still doubt your total forgiveness is a contradiction. Jesus Christ could never live in a person unless all of his sins were forgiven. He died *for* you so that He could live *in* you! His life in you is our assurance that you are totally forgiven and secure in His salvation.

It's impossible to receive Christ without receiving forgiveness of sins. It would be like offering you the pen separately from the Bible.

If you're struggling with your forgiveness, ask yourself if you are in Christ.

If you are in Christ, you can rest confidently in the fact that you have total forgiveness of sins.

Chapter 14

The Two-Sided Coin
of Salvation

*God made him who had no sin to be sin
for us, so that in him we might become the
righteousness of God.*

2 Corinthians 5:21

SALVATION, LIKE A COIN, HAS TWO SIDES. On one side is forgiveness, and on the other is righteousness. On one side God provided total forgiveness of our sins in Christ. On the other side, and equally as important, He gave to us His very righteousness. Both transactions make up the coin of salvation.

Many of us, however, view salvation only from the forgiveness side of the coin. It never enters our minds to turn the coin over to see what's on the other side. Somehow we have the idea that if we could just get all our sins forgiven, we would be wonderful people.

This isn't true. Having our sins forgiven doesn't make us righteous. We could quit sinning altogether and still not be righteous in God's sight. Righteousness (a right standing of total acceptability before God) is a gift that must be given to us.

The Bible declares, "There is no one righteous, not even one" (Romans 3:10). We have no righteousness of our own, and there's no way to become righteous by being good enough or by trying to live up to God's righteous standards. Romans 3:20 says "no one will be declared righteous in his sight by observing the law." So for us to be righteous in God's sight, we have to be *made* righteous.

Before we can be made righteous, however, we have to be cleansed of all our unrighteousness. That's the forgiveness side of the coin of salvation, and that is what Christ did for us at the cross.

First John 1:9 says, "If we confess our sins, he is faithful and just and will forgive us our sins and purify us from all unrighteousness." Jesus Christ went to the cross 2000 years ago and died for all our sins one time. And in so doing, He cleansed us from all our unrighteousness.

God, however, didn't simply take our sins and place them on Jesus. He also took Christ's perfect righteousness and gave it to us through His resurrected life—the other side of the coin of salvation. Second Corinthians 5:21 says, "God made him who had no sin to be sin for us, so that in him we might become the righteousness of God."

In Christ we have been *given* the very righteousness of God. As a result, we're as righteous and acceptable in the sight of God as Jesus Christ is!

We aren't righteous in God's sight because of what we've done. We're righteous because we've received the righteous One. His righteousness is a free gift to us when we receive Him by faith. Romans 5:17 puts it this way: "For if, by the trespass of the one man, death reigned through that one man, how much more will those who receive God's abundant provision of grace and of the gift of righteousness reign in life through the one man, Jesus Christ." This may sound too good to be true, but it is *the truth.*

Righteousness is a gift. No one can work for it or earn it. And no one deserves to be made righteous. Like any gift, righteousness can only be accepted or rejected. Once a person has accepted Jesus Christ, he or she has accepted His gift of righteousness and can say, "I am as righteous as Jesus Christ."

So remember, salvation is a two-sided coin. On one side is forgiveness; on the other is the righteousness of Christ. If you're in Christ, you're totally forgiven through Christ's death on the cross. And equally important, you've been given the righteousness of Christ through His resurrected life.

Today you can stand before God confident that you're totally acceptable in His sight—not because of what you've done, but because of what Christ has done on your behalf.

This, my friends, is the gospel—*good news*!

Chapter 15

My Dad, the Judge

He did it to demonstrate his justice at the present time, so as to be just and the one who justifies the man who has faith in Jesus.

Romans 3:26

PEOPLE FREQUENTLY ASK, "How can God be both just and loving at the same time?" For Him to be both seems like a contradiction to our finite minds. If He's loving, it seems He would have to compromise His justice. If He's just, then it seems He would have to withdraw His love.

In the cross, however, we see these two seemingly contradictory characteristics come together. In Romans, Paul describes Christ's death on the cross as both a demonstration of God's justice (Romans 3:26) and a demonstration of God's love

(Romans 5:8). It's much like the following illustration of the judge.

A young man was arrested for a crime. During the trial all the evidence needed to determine this young man's guilt or innocence was presented. The evidence was clear—the judge had no other option but to declare this young man guilty.

The judge slammed down his gavel and pronounced his decision: "Guilty as charged!" Then he imposed the maximum fine of one million dollars for punishment.

But then something truly amazing happened. The judge slipped off his robe, stepped down from his bench, and paid the young man's fine.

Why? Because it turned out that this judge was more than a judge. He was the young man's father. And his love for his son was so great that he was willing to pay the penalty for his son's crime.

In his doing so, the punishment for the crime had been executed, justice had been served, and yet the young man was free to go. The judge was both just and loving. As a just judge, he couldn't simply dismiss the crime. Otherwise, the law would have been compromised. As a loving father, he paid the penalty so that his son could go free.

That's exactly what God did for you and me. As our judge, He declared, "All have sinned and fall short of the glory of God" (Romans 3:23). His verdict is "guilty," and the punishment is death—"For the wages of sin is death" (Romans 6:23).

But God is more than our judge. He is our heavenly Father. In the person of His Son, Jesus Christ, He took off His judicial robe and went to a cross on our behalf to pay the penalty for all our sins.

God didn't compromise His divine justice. Our sin didn't go unpunished. Through the death on the cross of His Son, Jesus Christ, He paid the penalty for all our sins in full. Justice has been executed. Nor did He withdraw His love. As John writes, "Greater love has no one than this, that one lay down his life for his friends" (John 15:13). Jesus Christ laid down His life for us so that we could experience new life in Him.

God in Jesus Christ is just and loving. He demonstrated both through His Son's death on the cross. If you aren't experiencing the love of God, it's because you haven't fully understood the justice of God. Recognize that all of your sins have been judged and the punishment has been executed. Christ took it all.

When you understand this, you'll start the great adventure of growing in the love of God.

Chapter 16

Cleansed, Filled, and Sealed

God has chosen to make known among the Gentiles the glorious riches of this mystery, which is Christ in you, the hope of glory.

Colossians 1:27

In counseling sessions, both in person and on our radio broadcast, or wherever I encounter a Christian who's struggling, I ask, "Would you tell me your understanding of salvation?"

In almost every instance, the answer comes back, "Jesus died for my sins so I can go to heaven when I die."

Although this answer is partially correct, it falls far short of the total salvation God provided for us in Jesus Christ. Salvation is much more than forgiveness of sins; it's the imputation of life—*Christ's* life. Jesus didn't come simply to get people out of hell and into heaven. *His ultimate goal was to get Himself out of heaven and into people.*

Canning is an illustration that paints a perfect picture of salvation.

What's the first thing you do when you begin the canning process? You sterilize the jars, don't you?

Now, why do you sterilize the jars? Is it just to have a bunch of nice, clean, sterilized jars sitting around? What if your spouse comes home while you're sterilizing jars and asks, "What are you doing, honey?"

"Oh, sterilizing jars," you reply.

"What are you doing that for?"

"Oh, just to have some clean jars."

"What are you going to do tomorrow?"

"Sterilize more jars."

"Well, what are you going to do with those jars?"

"Keep 'em clean. Any time they get a speck of dirt in them, I'm gonna stick 'em under the water and get 'em clean again. I've sterilized them, and I'm gonna keep 'em that way."

"What are you going to do the next day?"

"Keep 'em clean—just keep those jars clean."

Your spouse would think that you'd lost your mind. You don't sterilize jars just to have a bunch of clean jars sitting around.

You sterilize the jars because you're planning to put food in them. And if the jars aren't totally cleansed of all impurities and you put food in them, what happens to the food? It spoils, doesn't it? So the reason for sterilizing the jars is so the food won't spoil or rot.

That's what happened 2000 years ago at the cross. God cleansed our "jar" of all unrighteousness. Why? So that He could have a bunch of cleansed vessels down here on earth? No! He cleansed us of all unrighteousness so that His life could fill us "without spoiling."

That's what salvation is: the imputation of new life. We've been cleansed once for all so that we could be filled with the very life of Christ. That's why Paul describes salvation in Colossians 1:27 as "Christ in you, the hope of glory."

It's interesting that once food is placed in the jar, the jar is described by what's in it. For example, if you put applesauce in the jar, it becomes a jar of applesauce. The identity of the jar is determined by what's in it. So it is with us. When Christ comes to live in us, we become children of God.

Once the jar has been filled with food, something else happens. The jar is then sealed. Sealing the jar is what keeps the good things in and the bad things that would spoil the food out. It's the final step in the canning process.

After we've been filled with the life of Christ, we too are sealed. Ephesians 1:13 (NASB) tells us, "In Him, you also, after listening to the message of truth, the gospel of your salvation— having also believed, you were sealed in Him with the Holy Spirit of promise."

The Holy Spirit is the guarantee of our salvation. Knowing that we've been sealed enables us to walk confidently in God's promise: "Never will I leave you; never will I forsake you" (Hebrews 13:5).

Cleansing, filling, and sealing—a wonderful picture of salvation. It helps us to see that salvation is much more than forgiveness of sins.

Jesus Christ cleansed us once for all 2000 years ago so that He could fill us with His life today. And once Christ has come to live in our hearts, He seals us with the promised Holy Spirit. Salvation, then, can be summed up in this statement: Jesus Christ gave His life for you, so that He could give His life to you, so that He could live His life through you.

What's important in canning is what's placed in the jar. Once it was just a jar. Now it's a jar of applesauce. What's important about salvation is that Christ has come to live in our hearts. Once we were just children. Now we're children of God. When we see that this is the true goal of salvation, the cross of Jesus Christ, where we have been cleansed once for all, takes on a whole new meaning.

I've seen literally thousands of Christians stop struggling in their experience once they understand that salvation is more than forgiveness of sins. If you're struggling in your Christian life, maybe it's because you've never gone beyond the forgiveness issue to see that salvation is life.

If this is the case, will you by faith accept that Christ's death cleansed you of all unrighteousness and that now the risen Christ wants to come and live His life in and through you? Once you see that completeness of salvation, you'll no longer have to struggle trying to keep your jar cleansed. Now you can go on to enjoy the life of Christ living in you.

You've been cleansed, filled, and sealed. The transaction is complete. Go on—enjoy the abundant life that God has promised!

Chapter 17

Stewart's Punishment

My brothers, I want you to know that through Jesus the forgiveness of sins is proclaimed to you.

Acts 13:38

FOR THE FIRST FEW MONTHS after the trial, Stewart felt that he had gotten off easy. After all, he had been responsible for the death of 18-year-old Susan in an auto accident.

He had been drunk and plowed into her car on a New Year's morning, killing her instantly. He was arrested and convicted of manslaughter and drunken driving. Then, on top of everything, Susan's family had filed and won a civil suit against him. But in their victory they requested an unusual and creative judgment. Though they had originally sued Stewart for $1.5 million, they settled for just $936.

However, those $936 were to be paid in a specific way. Each Friday, the day Susan died, Stewart was to make out a check in her name for one dollar and mail it to the family. The entire amount of $936 was to be paid one dollar per week for 18 years, one for each year of Susan's life. In this way, the girl's family was ensuring that Stewart would remember what he had done.

After his initial relief at the reduction of the judgment, Stewart discovered that this payment system was not the lark it first appeared to be. Very soon he began to grow weary of the ritual. Then it got worse. He found himself becoming depressed as he was reminded each and every Friday that he was responsible for a young woman's death. Writing her name on the check became more and more painful, so much so that he stopped writing them.

The family instantly went back to court to force him to continue. Four times during the next eight years Stewart stopped paying and was forced to start again by court order.

Finally, testifying that he was "haunted by Susan's death and tormented by the payments," Stewart went to court himself to appeal the "cruel" punishment that had been imposed on him.

In court he offered Susan's family two boxes of checks covering payments for the remainder of the 18 years, plus an extra year. The family refused.

"What we want," they said, "is to receive that check every week on time. We will pursue this until those years are completed, and we'll go back to court every month if we have to."

When I first heard of this real-life story from news reports, I immediately saw many gripping parallels to biblical truths. It illustrates pointedly why a Christian absolutely must come to an understanding of God's forgiveness and acceptance in Christ before he can go on to grow in grace.

Think about Stewart's situation. As long as he's required to remember his crime and continue to pay a weekly debt to Susan's family, what do you think are the chances that he could ever develop a positive *personal relationship* with them? None!

Writing that weekly check forces Stewart to concentrate on his past and produces continued guilt and regret. His cry is, "I just want to get on with my life," but his weekly ritual won't let him. As long as this is true, he'll want to stay a million miles away from that family. *You cannot enjoy a personal relationship when guilt stands between the parties.*

Read closely these words from the book of Hebrews:

> The law is only a shadow of the good things that are coming—not the realities themselves. For this reason it can never, by the same sacrifices repeated endlessly year after year, make perfect those who draw near to worship. If it could, would they not have stopped being offered? For the worshipers would have been cleansed once for all, and would no longer have felt guilty for their sins. But those sacrifices are an annual reminder of sins, because it is impossible for the blood of bulls and goats to take away sins. (Hebrews 10:1-4).

Over the years I've met many pastors and other Christian leaders who wonder why their people won't give themselves freely to God for His use.

It's no mystery to me. In many cases, it's because they're dealing with God on the same basis as Stewart is with Susan's family. They believe there's still some unpaid debt between them and God, and He must therefore be angry with them. As a natural result, they avoid Him. Their understanding of the forgiveness of their sins is more like the atonement offered under the Old Covenant than the completed work of Christ. They believe they are forgiven up to date, but they still owe on the balance.

When they commit a sin, they think, "Well, I blew it again. God's probably got His bottle of Pepto-Bismol out. He's up there, sick to His stomach at me." But God has a better remedy for sin than Pepto-Bismol. He has provided the cross as the final and sole answer to sin.

I like to state it this way: *Until you rest in the finality of the cross, you will never experience the reality of the resurrection,* which is Christ Himself living in and through you! Unless you rest in the fact that Jesus paid for *all* your sins, you'll be so busy trying to "pay off your debt"—atone for your sins—that you'll never grow as a Christian and enjoy the personal relationship that Christ has provided for you.

Stop right now and ask yourself: Is there any cloud of guilt between Christ and you? Is there some vague sense of not being pleasing in His sight due to your sins?

If you answer "Yes," then realize that you're not able to move on in Christ until you accept fully and finally that all your sins—past, present, and future—have been paid in full by Christ's death on the cross.

You are eternally forgiven.

Chapter 18

David's Dilemma

Be kind and compassionate to one another, forgiving each other, just as in Christ God forgave you.

Ephesians 4:32

I ONCE CONDUCTED A SEMINAR in a federal prison in Texas. With me were several volunteers to assist in counseling the inmates. One of the volunteers, named David, had been a believer for only about two years, but God's love had transformed his life. The cynical and hard construction company owner I had known had grown remarkably in grace. David had become a softhearted, friendly, and giving man under the influence of Jesus Christ. And now this young man was very excited to be working with the inmates at the conference.

Everything was going along just fine until my final lecture on the need to extend to other people the same forgiveness that we've received from God. What followed for David was a very unexpected and dramatic encounter.

David listened attentively, cheering me on in his heart.

"Yeah! Go, Bob!" he was thinking. "I sure hope all these prisoners are listening, because *they sure need this!*"

David was in that frame of mind, grinning and looking around to see if people were listening, when suddenly *he* turned and saw the face of the man whom he hated more than any man on earth.

Several years before David became a believer, this man had done some things to hurt him severely, both personally and professionally. In fact, David's hatred and desire for revenge at that time were so intense that, as he later told me, "The only thing that kept me from hiring a hit man to kill him was the fear of getting caught!"

Now here they were: This man was an inmate in a prison, and David was a Christian who had come to work with prisoners. David hadn't yet been noticed by this man he hated, and he knew he had to make a quick decision. The struggle in his heart was incredible.

Seeing that man for the first time in years had brought back all those hateful emotions in an instant—but David was a new man now. Jesus Christ had come into him, and had done tremendous things in his life; that was undeniable. But the memories and reactions of the flesh were still there.

"I knew what God's Word said about forgiving one another," he said. "But I wasn't ready for anything like this! Jesus' command to 'love your enemies' sounds like a beautiful sentiment until you actually have an enemy! What I wanted more than anything in the world was a way out of that room!"

But God was living in David, and was reasoning with him according to the truth.

"Even though I could look back at what this man had done to me," he said, "I also remembered that I hadn't been lily-white, either! The Lord had to do some serious forgiving in my life to make me acceptable to Him. Frankly, I couldn't see that there was very much difference between me and this other guy if you looked at us from God's perspective."

The war of emotions continued within David's heart, until I stopped speaking and announced a break. It was time to decide. A lot of David's feelings were still screaming about the old offenses, but God's love was also speaking to him. He decided to do what he knew God wanted him to do.

"I walked over and stood before him," David said. "And you should have seen his reaction! He nearly jumped out of his skin when he saw me. I think he expected me to slug him. Instead, I extended my hand and said, 'I hope you're listening to these messages, because Bob is right. Jesus Christ has changed my life, and He can change yours, too.'"

The man could hardly talk for a minute. Then he shook David's hand and said slowly, "If I didn't have a reason to listen before, I sure do now!"

David shared with me later that those old resentments were totally gone. The old hatreds were dissipated, and he feels a genuine compassion for a man that he once could have willingly killed.

How do you explain it? It's supernatural. Only those who have first *received* the love and grace of God can go on and become willing servants and "minist[ers] of reconciliation" (2 Corinthians 5:18) even to bitter enemies! The Bible says, "We love because he first loved us" (1 John 4:19).

When the message of His unconditional love and forgiveness in Jesus Christ is proclaimed, the power of God is unleashed in human relationships.

Part Four

LIFE

Chapter 19

Bridging the Gap

I tell you the truth, whoever hears my word and believes him who sent me has eternal life and will not be condemned; he has crossed over from death to life.

John 5:24

FOR THE LONGEST TIME MY EXPLANATION of the gospel centered solely on the forgiveness issue. If you had asked me as a Christian how I was saved, I would have answered, "Through Christ's death on the cross."

Down through the years I've often asked people, "What does it mean to be saved?" In most cases they reply, "Jesus died for my sins, and there will be a place for me in heaven when I die."

For a long time I used what I thought was an effective illustration of the forgiveness issue to help explain salvation. The illustration shows a person standing at the side of a cliff overlooking a deep chasm with God on the other side. In the illustration, the cross of Jesus is what bridges the gap and enables us to experience God's forgiveness.

In the past several years, however, I've discovered that the gospel is more than forgiveness. Now my illustration has taken on a new, even deeper meaning.

From the time that I received Christ, Romans has been one of my favorite books of the Bible. I've read it dozens of times. But during one of my readings, Romans 5:10 jumped out at me as if I'd never seen it before. It reads, "If, when we were God's enemies, we were reconciled to him through the death of his Son, how much more, having been reconciled, shall we be saved through his life!" I read this verse and asked, "Life? I thought we were saved by His death. What does life have to do with anything?"

But then I came to realize the importance of Jesus Christ not only dying for our sins but also His rising from the dead. I had understood what the cross of Jesus Christ meant, but I had no idea of the significance of His resurrection.

Sometimes we Christians are absolute geniuses at overlooking the obvious. What's the most obvious implication of the word "resurrection"? It's the *restoration of life!*

Perhaps you've had the experience of having a word called to your attention for the first time. Then you begin finding that word again while reading the newspaper, and in conversations, on billboards—seemingly behind every bush. You know, of course, that the word was there all the time; you were just unconscious of it. That was my experience with the word "life" in the Bible. Suddenly it was everywhere. It seemed as if God had sneaked in and rewritten the Bible when I wasn't looking.

Seeing the word "life" throughout the Scriptures brought to mind other Scripture references. For example, Ephesians 2:1: "As for you, you were dead in your transgressions and sins." This verse made me ask the question, "What kind of person needs life?"

The answer was obvious: only the dead. Before if I was asked what the problem of mankind is, I would have always discussed people's sinfulness and the need for God's forgiveness. This is certainly true, but the problem is much deeper. From God's point of view, the problem of people isn't just that they're sinners, but that they're dead and in need of life.

This brings us back to our illustration of how to explain the gospel. We aren't only standing at the edge of the chasm in our sins, but we're standing there also spiritually dead and in need of life. And the only spiritual life that's available for us is the life of God.

Before God could give us spiritual life, however, He had to deal with the thing that killed us in the first place.

When Adam came into the world, he was created alive spiritually. God told him he could eat from all the trees in the garden except for one, and that was the tree of the knowledge of good and evil. God told Adam that the day he ate the fruit of this tree, he would surely die. Through the temptation of Satan, Adam and Eve ate of the tree of the knowledge of good and evil. But they didn't die physically that day. The Bible records that they lived to be over 900 years old. How did they die then? They died spiritually. They were separated from the life of God. That's what death is: the absence of life.

Adam passed sin on to all of mankind. As it says in Romans 5:12, "Just as sin entered the world through one man, and death through sin...in this way death came to all men, because all sinned."

Every man and woman born into this world is born in the same condition that Adam was in after he sinned: spiritually dead.

What killed mankind? Sin!

So before God could restore back to us what we had lost in Adam, He had to deal with what killed us: sin.

Two thousand years ago Jesus Christ went to a cross and took upon Himself all of our sins. There He paid a debt He did not owe for us, who owed a debt we could not pay. Through His death Jesus took away the sins of the entire world, and as a result there's absolutely nothing that can keep us separated from the life of God except our refusal to accept His life through Jesus Christ.

We receive the life of Christ today by faith. When we simply put our trust in Jesus Christ—in the fact that He died and was raised from the dead—He comes to live in us through the Holy Spirit. Jesus Christ laid down His life *for* us, so that He could give His life *to* us, so that He could live His life *through* us. That's the gospel. We stand dead in our sins, separated from the life of God. God reaches across to us through His Son, Jesus Christ, offering us the very life that raised Jesus from the dead.

Have you recognized that the gap has been bridged in the person of Jesus Christ, and that all of your sins have been taken away through Christ's death 2000 years ago? Have you recognized you are dead in your sins and the only thing a dead man needs is life?

If so, are you willing to accept into your heart the same life that raised Jesus from the dead? Will you believe that the gospel is more than forgiveness of sins? As John 5:24 puts it, "Whoever hears my word and believes him who sent me has eternal life and will not be condemned; he has crossed over from death to life."

It's through the resurrection of Jesus Christ that any man, woman, boy, or girl on the face of the earth who comes to Him in faith receives His very life through the indwelling Holy Spirit.

That's how we live!

Chapter 20

How to Save a Drowning Man

Now there [were] many of those priests, since death prevented them from continuing in office; but because Jesus lives forever, he has a permanent priesthood. Therefore he is able to save completely those who come to God through him, because he always lives to intercede for them.

Hebrews 7:23-25

GOD CHOSE TO GIVE US eternal life. He could have given us temporary life or some other type of life. He chose, however, to give us *eternal* life. And this eternal life is in His Son, Jesus Christ. John writes:

> This is the testimony: God has given us eternal life, and this life is in his Son. He who has the Son has life; he who does not have the Son of God does not have life. I write these things to you who believe in the name of the Son of God so that you may know that you have eternal life (1 John 5:11-13).

81

Are you in Christ? Is He in you? Then what kind of life do you have? *Eternal* life! When does this eternal life begin? The minute you have the Son. How long is this life going to last? Forever! How long is Christ going to live? Forever! It's eternal life because it's *His* life. Therefore, how long are you going to live if you have the Son?

Many people, however, perceive salvation along a different line.

Let me illustrate. Suppose you're motoring along in your boat and see a guy out in the water drowning. Someone says, "Hey, that guy needs to be saved."

You respond, "That's obvious, but how do we go about saving him?"

"Oh, by our good example," comes the answer.

So you jump out of the boat and say to the drowning man, "Watch me swim." As you're demonstrating how to swim, you look over and see the guy going under.

"Obviously," you say to yourself, "you can't save someone by a good example."

Somebody else suggests, "You can save the guy through education."

This sounds good. So you find a book on how to swim and throw it to the guy out in the water.

"Just read this," you shout from the boat. "It'll teach you how to swim."

As the guy in the water makes an attempt to reach the book, he goes under the water again.

Education certainly isn't the answer.

Another person says, "Grab the guy out of the water, and put him in your boat. That'll save him."

Of all the suggestions you've heard, this one makes the most sense. So you paddle over to the drowning guy. Then you reach out and grab him and pull him in the boat. With a big sigh, you say, "Whew, I finally saved him." But is this salvation?

Not really, because as you're paddling to shore, the guy asks you for a cigarette. This makes you mad. You think to yourself, "This ungrateful slob. I saved his life and all he wants to do is smoke a cigarette. One more like that and back in the water he goes."

Then he says a cuss word. As a matter of fact, he starts cussing at you for not saving him sooner. This really makes you mad. So you pitch him right back in the water to drown.

Now was this salvation? Was the rescue complete?

No, it was merely a temporary reprieve. This is what so many people think concerning salvation—that they might do something to make God so mad that He will pitch them right out of the boat.

It's as if they think John 3:16 reads like this: "God so loved the world that He gave His one and only Son, that whoever believes in Him shall not perish but have *a temporary reprieve*."

Salvation is much more, however.

Salvation is when you grab the guy out of the water, put him in your boat, and deliver him safely to shore. Anything short of that is a disgrace to what God calls eternal life.

When God saved you, He grabbed you out of the water and delivered you safely to shore. He saved you completely. He didn't give you a temporary reprieve. He gave you His life, and His life is eternal. That's what salvation is—the imputation of life. Colossians 2:13 says: "When you were dead in your sins and in the uncircumcision of your flesh, God made you alive with Christ."

He didn't give you life because you were a nice person. Nor does He remain in you and you in Him because you act good. He saves you completely and delivers you safely to shore because He is faithful.

As Hebrews 7:25 states: "He is able to save completely those who come to God through him."

John said he wrote his letter so we would *know* we have eternal life. He didn't say, "I write these things to you who believe in the name of the Son of God so that you may *hope* that you have eternal life."

If you have the Son, you can know with confidence that you have eternal life. And because eternal life is something you didn't earn, it's something you can never lose.

Do you know that you have eternal life? Do you have the Son? If so, you can know that God has saved you completely. He'll never throw you back in the water.

Eternal life is yours to experience forever!

Chapter 21

At the End
of My Rope

We have this treasure in jars of clay to show that this all-surpassing power is from God and not from us.

2 Corinthians 4:7

Hᴀᴠᴇ ʏᴏᴜ ᴇᴠᴇʀ ꜰᴏᴜɴᴅ ʏᴏᴜʀsᴇʟꜰ in a situation where you almost felt like giving up? You may have tried everything in your ability to better the situation, but no matter how hard you tried, it just seemed to get worse. You probably felt like you were at the end of your rope.

I've heard people tell me many times during counseling, "I'm almost at the end of my rope!"

My response is, "Put some grease on that thing so you *can* get to the end of it."

This may not sound very sympathetic at first, but the truth is, that's exactly where God wants us to be. The only way we can experience His strength and sufficiency is when we stop trusting in our own.

Often we find ourselves in troublesome relationships with other people. It may be a boss who's not a Christian, an overbearing in-law, or a child who's a bit too active. Whatever the circumstance, our patience runs thin and we begin to get angry and bitter. We usually respond with, "Lord, just give me strength to endure this!" What we need to understand is that God doesn't want to help us with our patience or ability. He sent His Son so we could die to ourselves and trust *His* ability.

You can hold onto your own intellectual understanding or willpower. But sooner or later, given the right circumstances, these things are going to give out. You can either "let go of your rope" and trust Christ to work in and through you in the midst of the situation, or you can continue to hold on to your own resources, just hanging there, never experiencing true joy and freedom.

Paul wrote in 2 Corinthians 12:10: "I delight in weaknesses, in insults, in hardships, in persecutions, in difficulties. For when I am weak, then I am strong." In the midst of our day-to-day hardships and struggles, we can experience the peace and the strength that can come only from Christ.

Are you still hanging on to your rope? Are you still clinging to your own understanding and ability? If so, let go and allow the Lord to take control of your circumstance. That's why He sent His Son, who was without sin, to die in our place. Christ took the penalty for our sin so that, raised from the dead, He could live His life in us. He's the only one who *can* live the Christian life.

All He expects from us is simply to trust Him—to let go and let Him guide and direct us.

Chapter 22

Jean's Story

I am the bread of life; he who comes to Me shall not hunger, and he who believes in Me shall never thirst.

John 6:35 NASB

THE MOST FORCEFUL, LIFE-CHANGING POWER in existence is the message of God's unconditional love and acceptance in Jesus Christ. An unforgettable example of this is the story of Jean, a woman who had struggled all of her adult life.

Married to a career military man driven by ambition, Jean lived in many parts of the world. However, rather than enjoying an exciting lifestyle, Jean was plagued by continual depression. Through her dependence on prescribed medication, she tried to hang on to some sense of stability. But often even the drugs couldn't give her comfort in the face of the onslaught of depression.

On four separate occasions, the emotional pain drove Jean to attempt to take her own life. On her last attempt, she lingered for four days in a coma between life and death.

Her husband, tired of the burden of putting up with her, deserted and divorced her. After her fourth attempt at suicide, she was too frightened to try again. She resigned herself to living, trying to tolerate the continuing depression.

Alone, Jean returned to the United States to try to establish some kind of life. She settled in Dallas, where a friend invited her to a home Bible study that I was teaching.

When she was exposed to the good news of Jesus Christ and His love for her, Jean responded by immediately receiving Him as her Lord. She was amazed as she began to discover what God had to say about her in the Scriptures. She hung on every verse that talked of God's love and acceptance of her and of her new identity in Christ.

Her depressed appearance, tense nervousness, and labored movements began to be replaced by smiling bright eyes, calm relaxation, and a spring in her step. Jean's total preoccupation with herself was soon replaced by a genuine concern for other people.

Soon Jean's previous deep depression was only a memory.

I'll never forget the day Jean said to me with a beaming countenance, "Bob, all my life I've tried to kill myself, and I finally succeeded!" It was more than a little jarring.

Jean laughed at my expression and explained, "I was unhappy for so long. But now I've learned how much God loves me, and I'm learning more every day. That old Jean is dead and gone. She died at the cross with Jesus. But the new Jean is alive and perfectly loved in Him."

She went on to explain. "All my life I looked for someone to love me and to accept me just like I am. I tried to earn my family's acceptance. I tried to earn my husband's acceptance. I tried to earn my children's love. I tried to earn my friends' love. And all along I was even trying to earn God's love and acceptance. But it's terribly hard to make other people love you when you think you are unlovable. Only in Jesus have I found love and acceptance I can count on forever. But the wonderful thing is that since I quit trying to get people to love me, I have found more love than I could ever measure in God's other children."

More than five years have passed since I first met Jean. She's been absolutely free from depression every one of those five years. Today, Jean is a joyful, delightful Christian, full of compassion and love. She's a fine, sensitive, and wise counselor to other people who are in the same trap of depression and despair that she escaped through Christ.

Jesus said, "I am the bread of life; he who comes to Me shall not hunger, and he who believes in Me shall never thirst" (John 6:35 NASB).

Every human being born into this poor, sin-sick world is born with a craving for unconditional love and acceptance. When we humans learn to rely totally on Jesus Christ, we find Him to be just what He promised: the total satisfaction for that gnawing hunger and thirst. In Him we find unconditional love, unconditional acceptance, and meaning and purpose in life.

All searching comes to an end in Him.

Chapter 23

Grand Piano

We are God's workmanship, created in Christ Jesus to do good works, which God prepared in advance for us to do.

Ephesians 2:10

THE HUMAN SOUL IS LIKE a wonderfully built grand piano, a magnificent instrument. However, the quality of the music that comes from it is totally dependent upon who's at the keyboard. If a master concert pianist is at the keys, you'll be carried along in rapture from the beautiful music. But let a gorilla have a shot at that piano, and the result will be chaotic noise and actual damage to the instrument.

Why is this so? First, the master pianist understands the instrument before him. He's well acquainted with its intricacies and its wonderful possibilities for beautiful music. Second, he also knows how to play each note on the sheet of music before him. By striking just the right note at just the right time, a pleasing melody is created.

The gorilla, on the other hand, is ignorant of this large piece of furniture before him. He pounds the keys and hears noise without the remotest understanding of music theory. He just doesn't have any concept of how to use the piano in the way it was intended.

Just so, Christians face the daily choice of whether or not they will present themselves to Christ, the master pianist, who will produce the beautiful music of His life in and through them. Their other option is to present themselves to sin and self with the discord and destruction that it produces.

When Christ is controlling me, I love Bob George and the music God is able to make through me. But then I should expect only good music from allowing Christ to control me—after all He's the Master Musician. He understands me and all my potential because He created me for good works.

On the other hand, when I'm allowing sin to have control of me, I can't stand Bob George. I can hear the gorilla pounding the keyboard, and the resultant noise is ugly.

When we allow Christ at the keyboard, we're hearing the sounds of His life. The sound of the gorilla is the sound of death.

Who's sitting at the keyboard of your life?

Jesus Christ or the gorilla?

Part Five

IDENTITY

Chapter 24

In the White House

To all who received him, to those who believed in his name, he gave the right to become children of God.

John 1:12

THE ISSUE OF IDENTITY IS inescapable and central to our lives. We all ask, "Who am I, and what's my place in the world?" Tied in with this drive for identity are the spiritual needs of unconditional love and acceptance, and a meaning and purpose to life. That's why many people, Christians included, spend so much time and energy trying to discover who they really are—their identity.

Consider a small three-year-old boy, skipping down the imposing corridors of the White House. Armed servicemen, the best of the best, take no notice of the child who runs past their assigned posts. The boy passes several high-level staff members on his way, who likewise take little notice except for an occasional smile. Passing a secretary's desk, the little boy doesn't acknowledge her wave, intent as he is on his goal.

In front of the final large door stands another armed sentry. But the guard makes no movement to hinder the progress of the child, who opens the door and goes inside. With a grin, the boy runs across the carpet of the Oval Office and climbs into the lap of the most powerful man in the world.

Influential cabinet members wait to continue their discussion as President John F. Kennedy and his son, John-John, exchange good-morning hugs and kisses.

The years of the Kennedy administration are memorable to me because they were among the few times that there have been small children living in the White House. I remember seeing on the news how President Kennedy loved his children and delighted to include them in his day, even while attending to matters that concerned the future and safety of the entire world's population.

The contrast has always struck me: the most powerful man in the world—and the little boy who could stroll past secretaries, staff members, and security guards and bound into his father's arms. Can you imagine someone objecting: "Now, wait just a minute, little boy! Don't you know who that man is? He's the President of the United States, the leader of the greatest nation on earth. You can't just waltz in here anytime you want. And you certainly can't be sitting in his lap! Who do you think you are?"

John-John would have just looked up at his challenger with a surprised look. Then, with a grin of total confidence, he would have said, "He's my daddy!" You see, John-John knew who his father was, and his father knew who he was.

The tragedy of modern-day Christians is our utter ignorance of who we are in Christ. Jesus Christ has done everything necessary to make us acceptable to a holy God; He has given us His very life to experience every day. Yet too many of us still thrash around in doubt as to whether God will really hear our prayers, whether we're "worthy" to be used by God in the ministry, or simply whether God really and truly loves us.

"I mean, how could God love me, knowing what I'm really like?" we think in our hearts. I know from firsthand experience that these doubts haunt the lives of multitudes of Christians. I've heard them expressed time and time again in thousands of hours of personal counseling and teaching Bible studies.

I hear people each weeknight on live radio ask the same questions and express the same doubts. In seminars I've passed out index cards and asked the audience to write their answers to a single question: "How do you feel God sees you right now?"

The answers I've collected are pitiful. Here are some actual samples:

"A being that is a sinner, that tries not to sin, but ends up sinning."

"God must see me often as hypocritical. I've learned to play the role of 'Christian,' but my heart is not truly, fully yielded to God in every area of my life."

"He sees a very troubled and misinformed baby."

"I think He feels sick when He sees me: disgusted, disappointed."

"He is sickened at me."

It's not easy for people who think God is seeing them this way to apply verses like Hebrews 4:16: "Let us then approach the throne of grace with confidence, so that we may receive mercy and find grace to help us in our time of need."

At the heart of these people's needs, as well as John-John Kennedy's confidence, is the issue of identity.

Most people determine their identities through their appearance, occupation, abilities, family relationships, friends, denominational affiliation, and many other ways. The common denominator of all these human attempts to find identity is they're all temporal. They can change with the wind.

Professional athletes strike me as the ultimate example. Make a great play, and people will throw a parade for you. Blow the play, and they will likely hound you about it for the rest of your life.

The same thing holds true in marriage. If someone were to ask me, "What does your wife think of you?" my answer would probably be, "What hour?" It can change at any given moment.

Many people determine their identity by their profession: "I am a businessman," Mr. Executive says. But what happens when Mr. Executive becomes Mr. Fired or Mr. Retired?

Statistics show that a large percentage of men die within two years of their retirement. Why? Because what had been the source of their identity has been taken away from them, and they're no longer certain as to who they are.

"I am a mother," say many women. But what happens when the kids grow up and leave home to lead their own adult lives? Who are you then?

Christians who determine who they are by their outward talents are building their identities on sand. Athletes, models, and movie stars suffer injuries and illnesses that can take away their beauty or their strength. There's also the steady intense competition from the athlete who may play the game a little bit better than they do, or the musician who can play the piano better, or the model who is younger and better looking.

There's only one way to determine our identity that can never be shaken, one foundation that can't be taken away from us: our identity as a child of God.

While we're here on this earth, we might be a child of God who happens to be a businessman or a mother or an athlete. But the core source of our identity is our relationship with our God and Father. Only in this way can we ever begin to discover true security.

Our identity is derived from who we're identified with. When we were born into this world, we identify with our parents first. But our first parent on this earth ultimately was Adam. That being the case, we're all initially identified with Adam—fallen sinners, dead and in need of life. That's our first identity.

Our identity can be changed, however, through faith in Jesus Christ. When we come to Christ by faith, God gives us a brand-new identity: "To all who received him, to those who believed in his name, he gave the right to become children of God" (John 1:12).

As children of God, we can experience a personal relationship with God, our Father. Paul wrote in Galatians 4:6: "Because you are sons, God sent the Spirit of his Son into our hearts, the Spirit who calls out, 'Abba, Father.'"

"Abba" is the most intimate of Hebrew terms. It's similar to our word "Daddy." We can come to God calling Him "Daddy, Father."

No longer do we need to live in fear of God. As Romans 8:15,16 puts it, "You did not receive a spirit that makes you a slave again to fear, but you received the Spirit of sonship. And by him we cry, 'Abba, Father.' The Spirit himself testifies with our spirit that we are God's children."

No matter what circumstance we may be in, God's Spirit testifies to our spirit that we're His children. Knowing this enables us to approach God with confidence in our time of need.

The believer's identity in Christ isn't a side issue; it's central to experiencing the real Christian life. If we don't have a firm grip on our true identity, we won't have the confidence to go to our God and Father for help when we need it the most. But if we'll take a lesson from a little boy named John-John and rest in who we are, we can go boldly to the throne of grace and begin to discover the riches and freedom that we already have in Christ because we are children of the King!

If someone were to ask you who you are, what would you answer? If you're rooted in your identity as a Christian, I hope that you'd respond with confidence, "I'm a child of God!"

Chapter 25

Caterpillars and Butterflies

If anyone is in Christ, he is a new creation; the old has gone, the new has come!

2 Corinthians 5:17

WHAT DOES IT MEAN TO BE a new creation in Christ?

Does it mean that we used to do things like drink, smoke, or commit some other sin, and now we don't? Or does it mean something else?

Jesus told Nicodemus what it meant to become a new creature when He said, "You must be born again" (John 3:7).

To be made into a new creature means to be born of the Spirit of God. I like to describe it by using the example of a caterpillar becoming a butterfly.

Initially, a caterpillar is a hairy, ugly, earthbound creature. You can try to change the caterpillar by dressing it up, making it smell nice, or even educating it at Caterpillar University, but it's still a caterpillar. For the caterpillar to change, it must go through the process of metamorphosis.

To do this, the caterpillar weaves a cocoon in which it totally encases itself. Within the cocoon, the process of metamorphosis takes place. Then, a brand new creature emerges from the cocoon—a butterfly. Once ugly and ground-bound, the now-beautiful butterfly can soar gracefully through the sky.

In the same way, when you and I were born into this world, we were born under the law of sin and death. The Bible tells us that we're all sinners, separated from the life of God. We too try to look good, smell good, educate ourselves to act good, but underneath we're still sinners. For us to be made new, we must be born again.

This new birth happens when we place our faith in Jesus Christ. The Bible explains, "When you were dead in your sins and in the uncircumcision of your flesh, God made you alive with Christ" (Colossians 2:13). We pass from death to life and emerge a brand new creature with Christ living in us. "I have been crucified with Christ and I no longer live, but Christ lives in me. The life I live in the body, I live by faith in the Son of God, who loved me and gave himself for me" (Galatians 2:20).

We're new creatures because Christ lives in us. This means that we have the mind of Christ (1 Corinthians 2:16) and therefore have the ability to see life from God's perspective rather than man's perspective.

Alas, even after our new birth we may not always act like new creatures in Christ. Sometimes we land on things we shouldn't or forget we're butterflies and crawl around with our old worm buddies. The truth, however, is that once we're new creatures in Christ, we'll never be old sinners again!

Would it ever occur to you to refer to a butterfly as a "good-looking converted worm"? After all, it *was* a worm, and it was "converted."

But now it's a new creature, and you don't think of it in terms of what it was. It's simply no longer a caterpillar—it's a butterfly. We too were once sinners before we were born again. But God no longer recognizes us as sinners but rather as "saints."

That's why Paul addresses all of his letters to the "saints" and not to all the "old sinners saved by grace." Being a new creature in Christ means we have received a brand-new identity. And this new identity isn't determined by how we act. Rather how we act will be determined by our identity. The key to understanding this is to learn to see ourselves from God's perspective.

When we sin today, it's like the Lord brings a huge mirror and places it above us and asks, "Who are you?"

You look up and say, "A butterfly, Lord."

"Then why are you crawling around with the worms?"

"I don't know, Lord. It doesn't make much sense, does it?"

And then it's as if the Lord says, "I didn't make you into a new creature so that you could crawl around like a worm. I made you into a new creature so that you could fly with the butterflies. Get up and fly!"

Our new identity is now the motivation for our behavior. Paul tells us in Ephesians 5:8, "You were once darkness, but now you are light in the Lord. Live as children of light." A good paraphrase is "Once you were a worm; now you are a butterfly. Fly like a butterfly!" It just makes sense.

If you've come to Christ by faith, you're a brand-new creature—a saint in the sight of God. Christ lives in you. You don't have to *pretend* to be a new creature or *try* to act like a butterfly.

This is who you are. Recognize it and begin trusting Christ to live His life through you.

Get up and fly!

Chapter 26

The Parking Space

I do not understand what I do.

Romans 7:15

I HAD BEEN A CHRISTIAN for about six years, and had come to Dallas to head up a major citywide evangelistic campaign. I was working with some of the largest churches in America, hosting a daily radio program, and coordinating our efforts with local television stations. The atmosphere was continuous excitement, and I was right in the center of it all. I was beginning to think I was very close to reaching the ultimate in Christian maturity...until one day I took my wife, Amy, shopping.

It was a crowded, busy day at the shopping center, and it was hard to find a parking space. Therefore I thought it was my lucky day when I found not *one* but *two* empty spaces right in front of the store we wanted! But just as I was approaching my "answer-to-prayer" parking space, a guy driving a shiny new foreign car pulled into that spot and straddled the line, taking up both spaces.

At first I thought it was an accident. I rolled down my window and said nicely, "Sir, you probably haven't noticed, but you've taken up two spaces."

He gave me a quick glance and said with a smirk, "I know it."

As he got out of his car, I got a good look at him. He was middle-aged, with flecks of gray in his well-coifed hair. His shirt was open down the front, revealing numerous gold chains dangling over what looked like a "chest toupee."

I felt an instant and total dislike for that man.

A little more forcefully I said, "Well, would you please repark it, so I can use one of the spaces?"

Holding out his arm to escort a much younger-looking girl, he replied, "No."

At that moment all those years of being a child of God didn't mean a thing to me. My mood was now murderous. "Buddy," I said through clenched teeth, "if you don't move that car I'm going to stuff you in the tailpipe and move it for you!"

I started to get out of my car, fully intending to do what I said.

Amy looked at me as if I'd lost my mind, and said so. I told her that it wasn't my *mind* that I was worried about losing: It was that parking space!

Suddenly I stopped.

"What are you doing?" I asked myself. "You were perfectly willing, in fact, excited to give up your thriving, lucrative business to go into full-time ministry, but here you are ready to fight another person rather than give up that parking space!"

Having finally come to my senses, I spent the next several minutes maneuvering my car through the lot, driving mostly in reverse. My goal was to keep the guy with the foreign car from seeing my rear bumper—the one with the sticker that said "Smile! Jesus loves you."

Have you ever been there?

In spite of a sincere and genuine faith in Jesus Christ, have you ever suddenly found yourself acting in a stupid manner, as if you'd never heard of the gospel? If we're honest, we'll all admit to such times. All of us can forget who we are and what we believe in an unexpected moment.

We've all heard the inner voices, either real or imagined: "I thought you were a Christian!" comes the sneer. "I thought I was too," we respond in disgust. "How could I do such a thing?"

Let's be a little more pointed. Besides "unexpected moments," we all know that Christians can choose to live in a determined and long-term manner contrary to what God's Word says. In fact, we all have areas of our lives where we face ongoing struggles with temptation and failure. We sometimes wonder if we'll *ever* make progress in this Christian life.

Every believer I've ever known—with the possible exception of those who are brand new in the faith—has experienced what the apostle Paul described: "I do not understand what I do. For what I want to do I do not do, but what I hate I do....For I have the desire to do what is good, but I cannot carry it out. For what I do is not the good I want to do; no, the evil I do not want to do—this I keep on doing" (Romans 7:15,18,19).

This same conflict has been experienced by Christians of all ages, from every denomination, and from every geographical region.

We've all been put on guilt trips and brow-beaten to "give it everything we've got," but in spite of our sincere efforts, it just isn't enough. We just can't seem to get it right. Simply put, what we need is *life*. And that is exactly what Jesus Christ offers us: "I have come that they may have life, and have it to the full" (John 10:10).

In this painful process, one of the major truths that the Lord always directs us to is our *identity in Him*.

On the day I wanted to stuff that man in his tailpipe, God immediately worked in my heart, reasoning with me, "Bob, *who are you?*"

"I'm Your child, Lord," I thought.

"What does that mean, Bob?"

"It means that I'm totally acceptable to You, Lord. That all my sins are forgiven, even this one. And that I stand in the righteousness of Christ. He is in me and I am in Him."

"My son, in light of that, what sense does it make to lose your temper over a parking space? Which is more important, experiencing My life in you, or defending your own pride? Do you think I could possibly provide another parking space for you, not to mention anything else you need in this life?"

It surely seemed silly now. "Of course You can, Lord."

"Then remember who you are, and think of all the riches you have in Me. Trust Me."

And I did.

In the light of who I am in Christ, what sense *does* it make to act like that? None at all! The wonderful thing about the grace of God is that none of this reasoning is for the purpose of condemnation. It's simply to remind us of *who we really are* so that we can return to dependence upon Him. I had been a butterfly who lapsed back to acting like a worm for a while. The message was simple: "Get up and fly." Even though I didn't have the understanding that I do today, I can look back and see that God was reasoning with me in the same way.

"Who are you?", He continually challenges us. Then He reminds us to return to dependence upon Him and act in accordance with our true identity.

The believer's identity in Christ is a truth we'll find ourselves coming back to again and again as we grow in grace. *We never outgrow our need to be reminded of who we are in Christ!* It's something that God is trying to teach us from the first day of our Christian lives until the day we go home to heaven, and this truth provides a constant standard against which we learn to measure our thinking and responses throughout life.

Chapter 27

You're Rich

*P*raise be to the God and Father of our Lord Jesus Christ, who has blessed us in the heavenly realms with every spiritual blessing in Christ.

Ephesians 1:3

WHY ISN'T THE AVERAGE CHRISTIAN experiencing freedom in Christ in his or her daily life? I think it's directly related to lack of understanding of the riches he or she has in Christ Jesus.

One of the greatest illustrations I know of the importance of spiritual knowledge is the true story of a man named Ira Yates. Orphaned at age 12, Ira worked hard to make a decent living. Like many during those years he struggled to get ahead.

In 1915 Ira, against the advice of his friends and neighbors, bought some land west of the Pecos River that had been plagued by disputed boundaries, frequent droughts, and "greasy" water.

His good friend Nub Pulliam, who had once owned the property, warned him not to buy the land, telling him that "even the buffalo know better than to cross the Pecos [to that land]. Why even a crow won't fly over that land," Nub told Ira.

But Ira wouldn't listen. He bought the land, and for a long time it looked like everyone had been right. The land seemed worthless. Yates struggled, but eventually was unable to keep up the taxes on the land.

And then one day the Transcontinental Oil Company arranged with Yates to drill for oil on the desolate land. The first three attempts turned up empty. The land was no good. But then at the fourth well, the drillers struck oil big time. At a very shallow depth, they struck the largest oil deposit known at that time on the North American continent—a deposit that produced 80,000 barrels of oil every day! Overnight, Ira Yates became a millionaire.

Or did he? If you think about it, Ira had been a millionaire ever since he first signed the papers to acquire the land. The oil was always there. Ira just didn't know it. Even poor Nub Pulliam could have been a millionaire—if he'd discovered the true worth of what was his.

There are many Christians today who are living in the identical situation spiritually. The Bible tells us that God "has blessed us in the heavenly realms with every spiritual blessing in Christ" (Ephesians 1:3).

However, like Ira Yates (and worse, Nub Pulliam), most of us are unaware of the incredible riches we already have in Christ. We live our lives in spiritual poverty, struggling day to day, not experiencing the life and freedom He's provided.

But it doesn't have to be that way. There is oil on our property. God has provided an eternal inheritance for us, His children. In Christ we have riches far greater than those of Ira Yates. The day we came to the Lord Jesus Christ in saving faith, God gave us everything we would ever need "for life and godliness through our knowledge of him" (2 Peter 1:3).

Head knowledge isn't enough. The apostle Paul prayed in Ephesians that the "eyes of our hearts" would be opened. We need a true heart knowledge of God and the riches of His love and grace that are ours in Christ Jesus.

Are the "eyes of your heart" open to see what God has freely given you?

Do you realize that there's oil on your land?

Chapter 28

Childhood Scars

How ow great is the love the Father has lavished on us, that we should be called children of God!

1 John 3:1

ALL OF US CARRY THE SCARS from the past. Many of us remember painful childhood experiences only too vividly.

Just think of kids on a school playground. Remember how it felt to be the last one picked for the team? Or what about the nicknames: Porky, Sissy, Dumbo, Four-eyes, Stupid, Stinky, Pizza-face, Retardo. Perhaps even worse are the vindictive ethnic epithets: wop, kike, greaser, wetback—and the dreaded "N" word, aimed like a verbal assault missile at African-Americans.

Think of the labeling—even from well-meaning adults: "He's a slow learner." Or "What can you expect when you consider her home life?" or "Pretty good for a girl [or boy]."

Imagine the story of Susie, a little girl who colors a small picture with crayons and takes it to her mother. Mom oohs and aahs and says, "Susie, that's wonderful! You're a genius! I'll bet you're going to be an artist one day."

Susie goes away thinking, "If Mom liked that little picture so well, think how much she would like it if I drew a big one on the wall!" So off she goes, finds the biggest wall in her room, and proceeds with her masterpiece. A little while later, there's a shriek.

"Susie! You stupid kid! What were you thinking?"

This is very confusing to a child. One minute, you're a genius. The next minute, you're stupid. By the time we grow up, we've likely gained a lot of experience confirming that the opinions of other people are a shaky way to determine who we are.

Any of us can remember times as a child when we were given identities that were destructive. And many of us are still hurting and wrestling with those memories decades later.

Not long ago I was approached after a seminar by an elderly gentleman who was just beaming with excitement.

"I want to thank you so much," he said. "At this seminar I have learned for the first time who I am in Christ."

I asked him about his story, and he said, "I'm 87 years old. When I was a little boy, the other children called me 'monkey-face' and made fun of me. All my life I've struggled with my self-image. Now I can say that Jesus Christ has set me free!"

You're probably wondering what this man looked like. He was actually quite handsome! But for many years he had thought otherwise.

Our emotions will respond to what's in our minds, without being able to discern between truth and error. That's what happened to this man.

Can you imagine? For more than eighty years this man had been trying to escape being "monkey-face."

What a shame—and yet many people share similar experiences. As if the usual struggles for identity we all experience aren't enough, millions of people become labeled with an identity that focuses on their greatest weaknesses.

For Christians such an "identity crisis" is unnecessary. The goal of God for each believer is that he or she see his or her identity "in Christ." All of the qualities, all of the resources, all of the strength of Christ are available to every believer.

It's time to forget that nickname or false identity that you've been tagged with for so long.

You're no more worthy of being called that than Christ is.

Chapter 29

Ernie and Mike

*A*ll *of us who were baptized into Christ Jesus were baptized into his death.*

Romans 6:3

ERNIE AND MIKE GREW UP TOGETHER. They were fast friends as children—always playing together, always looking out for each other. But as often happens, as they grew older, their paths began to diverge, and they ended up in very different places.

Ernie was always in trouble. He began by shoplifting minor amounts of merchandise from stores and worked his way up to stealing cars. Next it was armed robbery. Finally, on one of his capers he killed a man. He was arrested, convicted, and sentenced to death.

Mike took a different track. He turned away from the rebellious tendencies of his friend and continued through school. He worked his way through college, graduated, and became a successful businessman. However, Mike had much difficulty with his physical health. His eyes in particular were weak. As he grew older, his eyesight deteriorated until he was legally blind.

One day Mike heard the news about his old friend Ernie. He felt a terrific compassion and sorrow for what had happened to his childhood friend, and he reached out to him. After exchanging letters to renew their old relationship, he went to visit Ernie in prison. They had a very touching and emotional reunion, speaking by phone across the security window at the penitentiary.

In spite of years of hard-hearted living, something in Ernie warmed as he talked with the man with whom he had played as a boy so many years before. And Ernie had an idea. Here he was, about to die while his friend had lost his sight. Was it possible, Ernie wondered, that he could do something worthwhile in his death? Could he give his eyes so his old friend could see?

It turned out to be medically possible, and when several months later Ernie was executed for his crime, his good eyes were used to restore Mike's vision.

This story has always intrigued me—a murderer's eyes being transplanted into the body of a law-abiding citizen. What determines the identity of those eyes? Whose were they before? They were a murderer's eyes. And now they allow Mike, a good man, to see.

Imagine this scene: A friend of Mike's comes up and says, "Hey, Mike, how are you? You're looking great...except..." He leans closer, squints, and exclaims in horror, "Do you realize that you have a *murderer's eyes?*"

"How stupid!" you'd say—and you'd be right. The character or behavior of the person who looked through those eyes before is absolutely irrelevant now. They belong to Mike. Those eyes take on the identity of the person in whom they live.

Like the "murderer's eyes" that were transplanted into the body of another man, the Bible teaches that you and I have been "transplanted" into Jesus Christ! Romans 6:3,4 says: "Don't you know that all of us who were baptized into Christ Jesus were baptized into his death? We were therefore buried with him through baptism into death in order that, just as Christ was raised from the dead through the glory of the Father, we too may live a new life."

The word "baptized" means to be "immersed in" or "totally identified with" something. In salvation, this is the work of the Holy Spirit in which He totally identifies a person with Jesus Christ. This spiritual baptism happens to every person who puts his faith in Christ—at the very moment he believes. Therefore 1 Corinthians 12:13 says, "We were all baptized by one Spirit into one body—whether Jews or Greeks, slave or free—and we were all given the one Spirit to drink."

Just as the eyes of a murderer were transplanted into the body of another man and therefore received a new identity, so guilty sinners are transplanted (baptized) into Christ and take on a new identity! It no longer matters what you *were*.

As far as God is concerned, the "old you" is dead and gone. That's what Paul meant when he wrote, "All of us who were baptized into Christ Jesus were baptized into his death" (Romans 6:3). "I have been crucified with Christ," he wrote in Galatians 2:20.

How can he say this? Because his old self (and ours)—previously identified as "in Adam"—has been considered executed through our identification with Christ at the cross.

My identity was once Bob George "in Adam"—spiritually dead, alienated from the life of God, a guilty sinner, and liable to judgment.

Where is that man, Bob George, today?

Gone forever! Now I am Bob George *"in Christ"*—a child of God!

If you've trusted in Jesus Christ, this is also *your* identity.

Chapter 30

The Prostitute Who Became a Bride

You were once darkness, but now you are light in the Lord. Live as children of light.

Ephesians 5:8

LET'S IMAGINE THAT A KING made a decree in his land that there would be a blanket pardon extended to all prostitutes. Would that be good news to you if you were a prostitute?

Of course it would. No longer would you have to live in hiding, fearing the sheriff. No longer would you have a criminal record; all past offenses would be wiped off the books. So the pardon would definitely be good news. But would it be any motivation at all for you to change your lifestyle? No, not a bit.

But let's go a little further with our illustration. Let's say that not only is a blanket pardon extended to all prostitutes, but also the king has asked you in particular to become his bride.

What happens when a prostitute marries a king? She becomes a queen. Now would you have a reason for a change of lifestyle? Absolutely. It doesn't take a genius to realize that the lifestyle of a queen is several levels superior to that of a prostitute. No woman in her right mind would go back to her previous life.

In the same way in Christianity, as long as a half-gospel continues to be taught, we're going to continue producing Christians who are very thankful they will not be judged for their sins, but who have no significant self-motivation to change their behavior.

But what's the church called in the New Testament?

The Bride of Christ!

The gospel message is in effect a marriage proposal. And just as the prostitute became a queen by marrying the king, guilty sinners have become part of the church, the betrothed of Christ. What a great change of identity—to be elevated from a life of sin to a life of royalty.

When we understand this love relationship and appreciate our new identity as the Bride of Christ, our motivation will change—and it's a change that comes from within as we learn to love our betrothed more fully.

When we understand that not only has blanket forgiveness been extended to us for our sins, but that we've also been offered a new identity as part of the Bride of Christ, our actions will change to correspond to our new identity.

Chapter 31

Janet's Story

You created my inmost being; you knit me together in my mother's womb. I praise you because I am fearfully and wonderfully made; your works are wonderful, I know that full well.

Psalm 139:13,14

A VIVID EXAMPLE OF THE IMPORTANCE of identity is the story of Janet, a young woman in her late teens who had been hospitalized several weeks for anorexia and bulimia. An anorexic person thinks she's fat and becomes obsessed with losing weight. Deceived into thinking she's still fat, she starves herself even when she has gotten to the point of looking like a living skeleton.

The bulimic part is the pattern of losing control of the diet. The woman gorges herself, feels guilty about it, and then forces herself to vomit the food to keep from gaining weight.

For six solid weeks Janet had been getting treatment for her problems in one of the leading hospitals in Dallas. But those treating her didn't consult what God has to say about human nature. Their diagnosis was that she had a "poor self-image" that needed improvement. Therefore they had her practicing Hindu meditation techniques which involved "catching the sunlight and bringing it into your body" to bring about healing, strength, and self-confidence. (And there are those who say you have to "put your brain in neutral" to be a Christian!) It reminds me of what God said, "Although they claimed to be wise, they became fools" (Romans 1:22).

After six weeks of failure, Janet's parents brought her to me.

I told them, "Leave her here for a few days. We'll let her do some volunteer work around the office, and I'll counsel her."

Less than a week later Janet went home, totally freed of her self-destructive behavior. How did that happen?

Not because I'm some super-counselor. Rather it's because truth sets people free.

Janet's problem wasn't a poor self-image—it was a total, obsessive preoccupation with herself. The answer wasn't a "positive" self-image. It was a *proper* self-image, based on truth.

As Janet and I dug into the Word of God together, we quickly identified that she was a typical Christian. She knew she was going to heaven when she died, but she had no idea how God loves and accepts her today, nor did she know about the life of Christ in her.

Without a solid foundation for determining her identity in Christ, she was forced to go to the world to determine it. And what does the world say? If you watch much television, you know the message: If you want to be admired by members of your own sex and desired by members of the opposite sex, you need to look like the models in the diet soft-drink ads.

If there is an ounce of fat on you, forget it. You'll be an unwanted nobody. Janet bought into this garbage as have many others.

It's a lie, but Janet became obsessed with trying to obtain the acceptance that the world offered—acceptance that's always offered with a string attached. It's always, "I'll love you if..." "I'll accept you if..."

That string always leads to bondage.

Janet and I talked about this error and looked into the Bible to discover what God said about her. She was amazed as she realized her total acceptance in Christ, and she responded immediately with joy and gratitude to her Lord.

Then we attacked the problem of her behavior.

"Janet, are you a bulimic or a child of God?" I asked.

After a pause she answered, "Well, I guess I'm both."

"No," I said. "You can't be both. God only gave you one identity. Which one do you choose?"

Then to help her understand, I asked her another question.

"If you *are* a bulimic, Janet, what's the most natural thing to do after you eat?"

"Throw up," she answered.

"So if you are truly a bulimic and the most natural thing to do is throw up, then why have you been going to counseling? After all, what you're doing is natural for a person who's bulimic—and don't you only go to counseling for doing something *inconsistent* with who you are?"

"I suppose so," Janet agreed.

"Well, if bulimic behavior is natural, then enjoy your throwing up! Go into a restaurant and have a meal and just splash all over everybody. Enjoy it! That's natural for you to do.

"But Janet, on the other hand, if indeed you're a child of God, then what would be the most natural thing to do after you eat?" I asked.

"Well, I guess get up from the table, having enjoyed the meal," she said.

"And if you're a child of God, what would be the most unnatural thing to do?"

"Throw up."

"So Janet, who are you: a bulimic or a child of God?"

"I'm a child of God."

"Then does it make any sense to continue doing what you're doing?"

She smiled and said, "No. Actually it sounds pretty stupid."

I agreed with her and continued, this time pointing her to a proper self-image.

"Janet," I said, "what does God say about you?"

"He says I'm holy and perfectly loved by Him," she replied.

"For how long?" I asked.

"Forever."

"Do you think God knew what He was doing when He made you? Do you think He could have made you differently if He wanted to?"

"Sure," she said.

"Then how much sense does it make for you to sit around all day, thinking about what's imperfect about you? To be thinking constantly about how much you weigh? Just to be thinking about yourself all day long every day? It's like saying to God, 'God, You don't know what You are doing. You can create a world all right, but You really blew it when You made me.'"

Janet thought a while. "It's really pretty dumb, isn't it?"

I nodded.

"Janet, no man is going to love you because you're as thin as a rake. Someone's going to love you because of the person you are. If someone accepts you or rejects you because of your waistline, then his love isn't worth anything at all. It isn't even love. Being preoccupied with yourself just makes you miserable.

"Jesus said, 'I didn't come to be served, but to serve.' We never find happiness by thinking about ourselves all the time. We discover real meaning and purpose in life when we learn to think about others and when we learn to serve other people. You're a butterfly, Janet!"

She gave me a big smile.

"Get up and fly!"

This is just an excerpt of our interchange. It wasn't a magical, instantaneous counseling session. But Janet did truly go free, and the answer was seeing her identity as a holy, loved child of God. That identity is a truth that the opinions of other people can't affect.

When Janet became dependent on Christ, who loved her and lived in her, she became free from her terrible bondage.

The believer's identity in Christ isn't a side issue; it's central to experiencing the real Christian life.

If we don't have a firm grip on this issue, we won't have the confidence to go to our God and Father for help when we need it the most.

But if we'll take a lesson from a Janet and rest in who we are, we can go boldly to the throne of grace and begin to discover the riches and freedom we already have in Christ because we're children of the King!

Part Six

LAW & GRACE

Chapter 32

Don't Get Stuck
in the Desert

There remains... a Sabbath-rest for the people of God; for anyone who enters God's rest also rests from his own work, just as God did from his.

Hebrews 4:9,10

WHEN I ACCEPTED CHRIST 30 years ago, my desire was to be "God's guy." Whatever He desired for me, whatever He wanted me to do, that became my mission.

People I looked up to told me that in order to be God's guy, I needed to witness, to pray, to memorize Scripture, to be involved in a local church. So off I went to get involved in every Christian activity possible.

I quickly became a "go-go" Christian, doing all the "right things" and at first loving every minute of it. But after several years, things changed. Instead of feeling like God's guy, I felt as if I were racing madly on a spiritual treadmill. I was highly active but going nowhere. What a contrast my life was to the "Sabbath-rest" that's talked about in the book of Hebrews.

My life reminded me of the story of Israel after Moses led them through the Red Sea. It was never God's intention that the Israelites linger in the desert. He told them to go straight to the promised land, where they could eat from trees they did not plant and drink from wells they did not dig. But because of their unbelief, they didn't enter into the rest to which God had called them. Afraid to go ahead and unable to return to Egypt, the desert was all they had left, with its boredom, monotony, and dryness.

Being engaged in so many activities, I lost the joy I had experienced when I first came to know the Lord and instead was enduring what seemed like a long trip in the desert. Every now and then a small voice in my heart would ask, "Is this really what the Lord Jesus had in mind when He talked about an 'abundant life'?"

Like the Israelites, I had a choice: I could either enter the Sabbath-rest God called me to—resting totally in the truth of His unconditional love and grace—or stay in the desert.

For almost eight years of my Christian life, I settled for second best.

God has prepared for you and me a Promised Land called a Sabbath-rest. Our rest isn't found in a geographical land but in our relationship with the living Christ.

God has always had a remnant of people who have said, "Lord, I'm not satisfied with the same old thing. I don't want to practice a religion; I want to know You in a real relationship." The hungry ones, the humble ones God will always lead into the Sabbath-rest.

This rest is described in Hebrews 4:9,10: "There remains...a Sabbath-rest for the people of God; for anyone who enters

God's rest also rests from his own work, just as God did from his." God wants us to grasp by faith that Jesus has done it all, and there is nothing left for us to perform to be acceptable to God. In other words, "God has done the work; now you rest!"

This "resting" isn't the same thing as being inactive. I can't think of anyone more active than Jesus Christ. Just as Christ rested in the fact that it was His Father doing His work through Jesus (John 14:10), so we too can rest in the truth that it's Christ living His life, doing His work through us. When we make ourselves available to God, we'll be more active than ever, but the work will be Christ's.

Are you roaming in the desert of spiritual activity, trying to make yourself acceptable to God? God has something better for you. It is called the Sabbath-rest. Don't settle for second best as the Israelites did, and as I did for eight years.

Enter God's rest. Rest from your works, just as He has rested from His.

Chapter 33

Spiritual Las Vegas

They devoted themselves to the apostles'
teaching and to the fellowship, to the breaking
of bread and to prayer.

Acts 2:42

HAVE YOU EVER WONDERED HOW Las Vegas came into existence? If you think about it, there really isn't any special reason for Las Vegas to be there.

However, a number of years ago a man from Los Angeles decided to put a gambling casino in the middle of the desert, in a place that contained nothing more than a gas station and a small grocery store. From those humble beginnings, and from the advantage of legal gambling in Nevada, Las Vegas has become a mecca for vacationers and fun-seekers.

But if you step back and look at the astronomical growth of Las Vegas, you quickly see the course of the human desire for more and more. The desire for gambling grew into a desire for entertainment. The desire for entertainment led to the desire for bigger and more spectacular forms of entertainment. Small hotels became big hotels. Big hotels became the ultimate in luxury.

They have built the flashiest, most exciting playground in America—as far as the world is concerned—right in the middle of the desert, in a place that no one would previously have wanted to visit, let alone live in.

If your intention is to excite and gratify the flesh, Las Vegas is just about the most glamorous place you can imagine. Now having said that, I want you to know it is not my aim to promote a weekend in Las Vegas, but to compare this phenomenon with the state of much of the Christian world.

We all know when the Jews were freed from Egypt they roamed in the desert for forty years before they entered the promised land. Sadly, much of Christianity has settled for *activity in the desert* rather than the *reality of a relationship* that is found only in Jesus Christ.

We are proud of our denominations and big buildings, our programs, our choirs and orchestras, and our ability to entertain and appeal to the emotions of the crowd rather than teach the truth that can be experienced only in the quietness of our hearts. These things of the desert keep us occupied for a while, but soon the arid surroundings take their toll, and we find ourselves searching for something more.

In my early years as a Christian, I was very impressed with and content with the glamour and the flashy approach to the Christian life. The desert was my home, and I didn't know there was anything different to be experienced. All the glitter quickly became old as I became disillusioned and burned out. My life had no real substance or meaning because my relationship with Christ was "one inch deep and nine miles wide."

In the Old Testament, Moses led God's people into the desert, but they never entered the promised land. Hebrews 3:19 tells us "they were unable to enter, because of their unbelief." It was not until Joshua (Joshua is the Hebrew name for Jesus) led his people across the Jordan into the promised land that they were able to enter into a brand new way of life. They ate from trees they did not plant and drank from wells they did not dig, enjoying by faith what God had provided—instead of living their lives to be entertained and pleasing the desires of their flesh.

Have you entered into the Sabbath-rest—the believer's promised land? There is only one way. His name is Jesus. Paul said, "I consider everything a loss compared to the surpassing greatness of knowing Christ Jesus my Lord, for whose sake I have lost all things" (Philippians 3:8). If you, like many of us, have substituted activity *for* Christ for resting in the total provision *of* Christ, remember there is a Sabbath-rest available through Him. "Let us, therefore, make every effort to enter that rest, so that no one will fall by following their example of disobedience" (Hebrews 4:11).

To the "poor in spirit," God will always respond by leading them to true freedom. Jesus gave us the assurance: "Ask and it will be given to you; seek and you will find; knock and the door will be opened to you" (Matthew 7:7). We can do this knowing that God "is able to do immeasurably more than all we ask or imagine, according to his power that is at work within us" (Ephesians 3:20). The writer of Hebrews describes this life as a "Sabbath-rest."

In the beginning, God created everything in six days, "so on the seventh day he rested from all his work" (Genesis 2:2). In Hebrews 4:9,10 the spiritual meaning of this pattern is explained: "There remains...a Sabbath-rest for the people of God; for anyone who enters God's rest also rests from his work, just as God did from his."

When we've entered into that rest—trusting in the complete and finished work of Christ—we're urged to go forward aggressively, laying hold of all that God has prepared for us. We're called to grow in grace.

The first true Christians understood this. They had spent long enough in the desert of religion. When they met Christ, they put away their traditions and devoted themselves to what truly mattered—to the apostles' teaching and to the fellowship, to the breaking of bread and to prayer.

Come out of the emptiness and artificiality of living in spiritual Las Vegas, just as the early church did. There is something better open to us and waiting for us.

Chapter 34

The Old and the New Don't Mix

Neither do men pour new wine into old wineskins. If they do, the skins will burst, the wine will run out and the wineskins will be ruined. No, they pour new wine into new wineskins, and both are preserved.

Matthew 9:17

THERE'S THE MISTAKEN BELIEF among some Christians that "God's grace gives us the ability to live up to God's law."

Such believers acknowledge that we're saved by grace and might even call someone a heretic who said otherwise. But when it comes to living the Christian life, they think that it's done through obedience to the law. But what they're doing is what I call co-mingling law and grace.

This isn't a new problem. Paul addressed it throughout his letters, primarily in the book of Galatians. As a matter of fact, the mixing of law and grace is commonly referred to as "Galatianism."

Jesus addressed this and showed the damage it causes by giving an illustration of pouring new wine into old wineskins.

Some of Jesus' critics asked Him why His disciples weren't observing all the legalistic traditions that had been passed down through the generations. Specifically they wanted to know why His disciples weren't fasting.

Jesus responded: "Neither do men pour new wine into old wineskins. If they do, the skins will burst, the wine will run out and the wineskins will be ruined. No, they pour new wine into new wineskins, and both are preserved" (Matthew 9:17).

In the winemaking process of Jesus' day, after the grapes had been picked and the juice squeezed out of them, the liquid was poured into a new wineskin. In the wineskin, this new wine fermented, producing a gas that expanded and stretched the wineskin to its capacity. Once the skin had been stretched, it was never used again.

If it were, the new wine would stretch the old wineskin beyond its capacity. The wineskin would burst, and both the wine and the wineskin would be lost. That's what we do when we mix law and grace; we ruin the purpose of each. We rob the law of its terror and condemnation, and rob grace of its freedom, joy, and life.

It's important for us to realize that the major division in the Bible is the one between law and grace. This division is seen in John 1:17: "The law was given through Moses; grace and truth came through Jesus Christ." And what was given through Moses (law) has a totally separate and distinct purpose from that which comes through Jesus Christ (grace and truth).

The law was given to Moses at Mount Sinai after the Israelites crossed through the Red Sea to escape their bondage in Egypt. God gave the law to Israel for their protection. This law, however, has a purpose in our lives on a spiritual level. Paul writes throughout his letters that the purpose of the law is to convict us of our need for salvation and then point us to Jesus Christ so that we might have salvation in Him. This makes sense. Why would we ever turn to Christ for salvation if we didn't know that we needed salvation?

So the law does its work by pointing out our sinfulness (Romans 3:20); by showing us that apart from Christ we are dead in our sins (Romans 7:9,10); and then as Galatians 3:24 states, "The law was put in charge to lead us to Christ that we might be justified by faith." That's the purpose of the law. And once the law has done its work, Galatians 3:25 says, "Now that faith has come, we are no longer under the supervision of the law."

Paul couldn't have made this point any clearer: The law has no place in the believer's life. Paul restates this in Romans 6:14 where he says, "You are not under law, but under grace." As Christians, we live under the grace of God—the grace that came through Christ Jesus.

God didn't intend for us to try to live up to the standards of the law. He knew that it would be an impossibility for us. In our pride, however, we think that we can keep the law. But because we can't, the law continues to condemn us by showing us our sinfulness. That's what Paul meant when he said in Galatians 2:18, "If I rebuild what I destroyed, I prove that I am a law-breaker." The law condemns us before our salvation. And if we try to live up to it as Christians, it continues to condemn us. That's the law's purpose.

It's no wonder then that so many Christians live defeated lives. They're trying to live up to something that was meant to condemn and kill them. If we're going to experience the abundant life Jesus promised, then we must die to the law and come alive to the grace of God.

The grace that saves us is the same grace that sustains us in our Christian life. Paul in his Christian life learned that God's grace is enough. In 2 Corinthians 12:9, God told him, "My grace is sufficient for you."

God's grace gives us life (Ephesians 2:4,5), enables us to go through testing and suffering, and teaches us to say no to unrighteousness and "live self-controlled, upright and godly lives in this present age" (Titus 2:12). It only takes a little bit of the law, however, to ruin God's purpose in grace. You can't mix the two. The new wine of grace cannot be contained in the old wineskin of law.

Hear what Paul had to say to those who co-mingled law and grace:

> You foolish Galatians! Who has bewitched you? Before your very eyes Jesus Christ was clearly portrayed as crucified. I would like to learn just one thing from you: Did you receive the Spirit by observing the law, or by believing what you heard? Are you so foolish? After beginning with the Spirit, are you now trying to attain your goal by human effort? (Galatians 3:1-3).

Like the Galatians, are you trying to live the Christian life through self-effort? If so, are you willing to recognize that the law has done its work in your life—that it has pointed out your sinfulness and your need for Christ? Are you willing to recognize that as a child of God you're no longer under the law, but under the grace of God?

If you're in Christ, the law is not for you. First Timothy 1:8,9 says that the law is for the unrighteous, for the lost. Therefore, are you willing to die to the law, and come alive to the grace of God? "For through the law I died to the law so that I might live for God" (Galatians 2:19).

If you *are* willing, your life will never be the same.

Chapter 35

The Mirror of the Law

The law was put in charge to lead us to Christ that we might be justified by faith. Now that faith has come, we are no longer under the supervision of the law.

Galatians 3:24,25

WHAT'S THE PURPOSE OF THE Old Testament law? The answer to this question is one of the most important and yet most misunderstood principles of the Christian life.

"Aren't we to be led by the law in our daily lives as Christians?" is a question I'm often asked.

My answer is always a resounding, "No!"

The law is for the lost, not the saved. Scripture says, "We also know that law is made not for the righteous but for lawbreakers and rebels, the ungodly and sinful" (1 Timothy 1:9).

138

In its proper role, the law provides a means by which people can see their true spiritual condition. The law is like a mirror. The mirror can show you that your face is dirty, but it can't wash your face for you. So it is with the law. It shows us that we're sinful and spiritually dead, but offers no solution to either.

Not only do we see our hopeless condition, but we also realize we're like a man without arms. We see our reflection and our need for cleansing, but we're helpless to do anything about it. If our face is going to get cleansed, then someone else will have to do the job. That's why Galatians 3:24 says that the purpose of the law is to lead us to Christ.

Why does it lead us to Christ? Because the law is powerless to save us.

> A man is not justified by observing the law, but by faith in Jesus Christ. So we, too, have put our faith in Christ Jesus that we may be justified by faith in Christ and not by observing the law, because by observing the law no one will be justified (Galatians 2:16).

Not only is it impossible for the law to produce righteousness, neither can it give life: "I found that the very commandment that was intended to bring life actually brought death" (Romans 7:10).

The law demands perfection. Since we're all born in sin, it's impossible for anyone to live up to the perfection of the law. Our only hope is to turn to Christ who alone can redeem us. If the law has done its work (led us to Christ) and as a result faith has come, then the purpose of the law has been perfectly fulfilled. Therefore if we've been justified by grace through faith, "now that faith has come, we are no longer under the supervision of the law" (Galatians 3:25).

When we—by faith—accept Christ's once-for-all payment for sin and receive His very life, our identity is no longer that of a filthy, wretched sinner. Our new identity is that of a child of God—a forgiven saint. We no longer have to live by law to try to make ourselves acceptable to God—an impossible task anyway. Because of Christ, we've been made acceptable before God *regardless of our actions*.

So what place does the law have? Its place is to show us our sinfulness in comparison to the righteous requirements of a holy God. When the law has done its work and led us to Christ, then it has fulfilled its function and purpose, and we never need to look into that mirror again. We're now led inwardly by the Holy Spirit.

Are you resting in what Christ has already done for you, or are you trying to make yourself acceptable to God by living under law?

Stop trying to look in the mirror of the law—turn to Christ and see yourself as you *really* are—from *His* perspective.

Chapter 36

The City Dog and the Country Dog

Through the law I died to the law so that I might live for God.

Galatians 2:19

In Titus 2:12,13 Paul declares that the grace of God "teaches us to say 'No' to ungodliness and worldly passions, and to live self-controlled, upright and godly lives in this present age, while we wait for the blessed hope—the glorious appearing of our great God and Savior, Jesus Christ."

For some reason we don't believe that it is the grace of God which is teaching us to say no. We think that it is our obedience to the law which produces godly living.

The law we follow isn't necessarily the Ten Commandments, either. We even make up our own rules and regulations for godly living. The Bible tells us, however, that the power of sin is the law (1 Corinthians 15:56). What we think will produce godly living actually does the opposite. It's no wonder so many Christians live defeated lives and many either give up or totally rebel. The difference between what the law produces and what the grace of God produces in our lives reminds me of the difference between a city dog and a country dog.

A city dog has a good life. He's got his own doghouse in the backyard. Normally he has a full bowl of water. He's fed a couple of times a day. He can sleep all day if he wants. He gets patted on the head and scratched behind the ears. This city dog is well taken care of.

With all the comforts at his disposal in the backyard, you'd think that the city dog would want to stay at home. But what does this city dog live to do? To get outside the fence!

All you have to do is crack the gate just a little, and you'll see a black nose squeezing through. If you aren't on your toes, the dog is out the gate before you know what's happened. Then he runs. Of course you try to catch the dumb thing, but the faster you run the faster he goes. And if he's like my dog, he looks back at you with his tongue hanging out like he's laughing at you.

You can ask yourself, "What's wrong? This dog has a great life." But the problem is the fence. The dog may have a pretty good life in the backyard, but he's not free. Because he isn't free, all he wants to do is get out.

That's what happens when we try to live under the law. It feels like we're living inside a fence. On the surface, we may look as if we have a pretty good life. But on the inside, there's no freedom. The reason is that it's impossible to live up to the law—or any set of rules and regulations. And the harder we try, the more condemned and in bondage we feel. Eventually we become like the city dog, living for nothing but to get out from under the law.

By contrast, go out to a farm where there are no fences. Where do you find the country dog? On the front porch...all day long. You can't get the dumb thing off. There aren't any fences. He's free and can go any place he wants, but all he wants to do is lie on the porch of his master, waiting for him to come out, pet him on the head, and put him in the pickup and take him somewhere.

He's content just resting at the foot of his master.

Why? Because there are no fences. A country dog is totally free. He could run all over the farm if he so desired. Yet he chooses to rest on his master's porch.

That's what the grace of God does in our lives. Under the grace of God, we have total freedom to do whatever we so desire. First Corinthians 6:12 tells us, "Everything is permissible."

Knowing that we're free, however, doesn't make us live like the city dog. It makes us approach life like the country dog. You see, it's the grace of God that knocks the fences down and enables us to fall in love with our Master.

That's the difference between law and grace. God never intended for us to live under the law. As a matter of fact, He says those who are under the law are under a curse: "All who rely on observing the law are under a curse, for it is written: 'Cursed is everyone who does not continue to do everything written in the Book of the Law'" (Galatians 3:10). He gave us the law to condemn us and point us to the grace of God found in Jesus Christ. And as Galatians 3:25 states: "Now that faith has come, we are no longer under the supervision of the law."

We're no longer under the law because the law can't produce the Christian life. Only the grace of God can do that.

In your own life you must decide whether you will live under law or under grace.

Paul said, "I do not set aside the grace of God, for if righteousness could be gained through the law, Christ died for nothing!" (Galatians 2:21). Are you setting aside the grace of God by believing that it takes the law to produce godly living?

If so, are you willing to die to the law and rest confidently in the grace of God to teach you to say "No!" and to live a righteous, upright life?

You can continue to live as a city dog cooped up inside a fence, or you can live as a country dog, totally free and resting at the foot of the Master.

It's your choice.

Chapter 37

Corks Under Water

*F*or Christ died for sins once for all, the righteous for the unrighteous, to bring you to God.

1 Peter 3:18

As STRANGE AS IT MAY SOUND to you, the goal of the Christian life is not to *stop sinning*, but to *start trusting*. The law shows us our unrighteousness—but the grace of God not only teaches us to say no to unrighteousness, but also teaches us how "to live self-controlled, upright and godly lives in this present age, while we wait for the blessed hope—the glorious appearing of our great God and Savior, Jesus Christ" (Titus 2:12,13).

When your emphasis in life is only on how to stop sinning, you will never get around to learning how to start living. It is much like trying to hold ten corks under water at the same time.

By the time you get five of them under water, the five others have popped up. In other words, trying to keep sin out of your life is an exercise in futility.

Someone once said to me, "Oh, I could never commit murder." My reply was, "If that is true, then you only need 90 percent of Jesus. If you could never murder and also never commit adultery, then you would only need an 80-percent Jesus. Just think—you may grow to the point in your Christian life where you would not violate *any* of the ten commandments, and then you would not need Jesus at all."

The idea that a believer could ever reach sinless perfection is an idea contrary to the revealed Word of God. There will never come a time in our lives when we will need less than *100-percent dependence* upon Jesus.

As long as we are living in this flesh that is indwelt by sin, we will always be subject to the temptations of sin and the possibility of giving into that sin. God did not come to take sin out of our flesh. He came to control the flesh by His Spirit. Paul puts it this way, "Walk by the Spirit, and you will not carry out the desire of the flesh" (Galatians 5:16 NASB).

Therefore, the emphasis of the Christian life is on learning how to walk in love, which is the fulfillment of the law. "For sin shall not be your master, because you are not under law, but under grace" (Romans 6:14).

The opposite of this verse is also true. When we are under the law, sin is our master. We as believers cannot be led by two masters. If you are under the law, sin is your master. If you are led by the Holy Spirit, Jesus is your master. We are to be led by the law of love.

Jesus has dealt with sin once and for all. And as the writer of Hebrews states, "he will appear a second time, not to bear sin, but to bring salvation to those who are waiting for him"

(Hebrews 9:28). Why isn't He coming to bear sin? He already has—and He cried out at the cross, "It is finished!"

As long as we concentrate on trying to keep our corks (sins) under the water, we will never offer ourselves to God so we can walk in love and be used to comfort the lost. Why should we focus on our sins? God Himself keeps no record of our wrongs—and we know "there is now no condemnation for those who are in Christ Jesus, because through Christ Jesus the law of the Spirit of life set me free from the law of sin and death" (Romans 8:1,2).

Chapter 38

People and Shadows

The law is only a shadow of the good things that are coming—not the realities themselves.

Hebrews 10:1

PICTURE YOURSELF ON A BEAUTIFUL WHITE sandy beach with the sun high in the sky.

When you're standing with the sun behind you, what do you see in front of you?

A shadow, right?

And who is it a shadow of?

It's a shadow of you. But the shadow isn't the real you.

This is how the Bible describes the law. Hebrews 10:1 tells us, "The law is only a shadow of the good things that are coming—not the realities themselves." What is so sad in modern-day Christianity is that many believers would rather live according to the shadow than experience the reality.

But the law, like a shadow, is powerless. For example, the law required a bull and a goat to be sacrificed each year to atone for the sins of the people, in an elaborate ritual performed by the High Priest. Jews traveled from all over Israel to Jerusalem to participate. After it was all said and done, the sins of the people had been taken care of—for that year. The problem was that sins started "clicking off" again the next day, and the people would have to wait yet another full year before atonement could be made again.

The blood of bulls and goats could *atone* for sin, but it did not have the power to *take away* sin and provide real forgiveness to the people. The writer of Hebrews declares its inadequacy: "For this reason it [the law] can never, by the same sacrifices repeated endlessly year after year, make perfect those who draw near to worship. If it could, would they not have stopped being offered? For the worshipers would have been cleansed once for all, and would no longer have felt guilty for their sins. But those sacrifices are an annual reminder of sins, because it is impossible for the blood of bulls and goats to *take away sins*" (Hebrews 10:1-4 emphasis added).

The word "atone" means "to cover." Atonement is like a credit card. The credit card can cover the cost of an item you purchase, but it cannot take away the debt you owe. Under the old system, forgiveness could never be a reality, because the debt was never paid.

In contrast, Jesus came as the "Lamb of God, who takes away the sin of the world" (John 1:29)! His sacrifice did more than merely cover our sins. He paid our debt in full and as a result took away our sins forever. Today, we stand in Him as forgiven people. The *reality* of forgiveness is ours.

In some translations of the Bible, the word "atonement" has been dragged from the Old Covenant into the New to describe what Jesus did. However, atonement is not a New Testament word. When you see the word "atonement" in the New Testament, look for a footnote at the bottom of the page. There you will see the real word is "propitiation." This means that Jesus, through His sacrifice on the cross, turned aside the wrath of God, taking away all of our sins. He satisfied the wrath of God on our behalf.

Today, we do not have to wonder whether or not our sins are forgiven, or wait for that day when another sacrifice will be made. Jesus died one time for all sin. As Paul states in Colossians 2:14, "*He forgave us all our sins,* having canceled the written code, with its regulations, that was against us and that stood opposed to us; he took it away, nailing it to the cross" (emphasis added).

So—back to our beach: Where is your shadow when you turn and face the sun? It's behind you, isn't it? If you are going to experience the reality of forgiveness in your life, you must put the law behind you by turning and facing the Son.

Part
Seven

DEPENDENCE

Chapter 39

For Me to Live Is Mom

For to me, to live is Christ.

Philippians 1:21

GOD HAS PROVIDED NUMEROUS illustrations on a physical level to help us understand spiritual truth. One such illustration that is especially meaningful to me was provided through the birth of my grandson, Robert.

When my two children were born, I was so wrapped up in my business that I missed much of the childbirth experience. With little Robert, however, I was very interested in learning everything I could about the development of this new life.

My son-in-law, John, is a physician. Through my conversations with John, I learned a lot about pregnancy, childbirth, and babies that I didn't know before. The more we talked, the more fascinated I became with the whole childbirth process. What really caught my attention, however, was the baby's growth inside the mother.

Inside the womb, the baby is totally surrounded by water. A baby surviving in water! How could this be? Fish live in water, not humans.

I jokingly asked, "Debbie's not going to have a fish, is she?"

The baby survives in this sack of water because it's attached to its mother by the umbilical cord, through which the mother provides everything the baby needs. The life of the baby is sustained through the life of the mother.

If the mother stopped breathing, so would the baby. If the mother's heart stopped beating, so would the baby's. If the mother didn't eat, the baby wouldn't receive nourishment. The baby is totally dependent upon its mother. Because of this dependent relationship on the mother, the baby in the womb could say, "For me to live is Mom."

This parallels our relationship with Christ. In this world, we're totally dependent upon Jesus Christ for our very life. Paul writes in Colossians that Christ *is* our very life. And John writes that Jesus said, "Because I live, you also will live" (John 14:19). If He were to lose His eternal life, we would lose our eternal life. His very life is what sustains us.

We experience Christ's life through the Holy Spirit. Like the umbilical cord, He's our lifeline. Through the Holy Spirit, Christ provides us everything we need to experience the abundant life He promised. Therefore, like the baby in the womb, we can say, "For to me, to live is Christ" (Philippians 1:21).

This is the attitude Christ wants each of us to adopt. The Christian life is a life of dependence. While on earth, Jesus demonstrated this life of dependence. In John 5:30 Jesus said, "By myself I can do nothing." Certainly, as God, Jesus could and can do all things, but when the "Word became flesh," Jesus chose to live as a man.

As a man, Jesus lived in total dependence upon His Father. He did nothing on His own initiative. When He spoke, He said what the Father told Him to say (John 8:28). In the same way, He did only what the Father told Him to do (John 5:19). He described this life of dependence in John 14:10 when He said, "It is the Father, living in me, who is doing his work."

Just as Jesus lived in total dependence upon His Father, we're to live in total dependence on Jesus Christ. That's why Paul wrote, "I have been crucified with Christ and I no longer live, but Christ lives in me. The life I live in the body, I live by faith in the Son of God, who loved me and gave himself for me" (Galatians 2:20).

It's Christ who lives in us and is doing His work. Our role is to live by faith and adopt an attitude of total dependence upon Christ to live His life through us.

For me there's no better illustration of the Christian life than a baby in the womb. It can truly say, "For me to live is Mom." This is a constant reminder that my life is derived from Jesus Christ.

If you are in Christ and Christ is in you, you can say of Him, as can the baby of its mother, "For me to live is Christ."

Chapter 40

Floating

I have been crucified with Christ and I no
longer live, but Christ lives in me. The life I
live in the body, I live by faith in the Son of
God, who loved me and gave himself for me.

Galatians 2:20

HAVE YOU EVER *tried* to float?

If you have, you know that the harder you try, the faster you
sink.

Have you *tried* to live the Christian life?

It's just like trying to float. It seems impossible! The harder
you try to live the Christian life, the worse you do. The key to
both, however, is in not trying at all.

My dad taught me the key to floating when I was a kid. On
our summer vacations to the beach, he spent most of his time
floating in the ocean. He stretched out, put his arms behind his

head, and floated for hours at a time. Every time I tried, however, I sank right to the bottom.

"Dad, how do you do that?" I asked.

His answer was, "I'm not actually doing anything at all. I'm just relaxing out there."

After numerous attempts to float, I finally learned the key. My job was merely to surrender my body to the water. *It was the water's job to hold me up.*

So it is with the Christian life. *We* can't live the Christian life; only *Christ* can.

Paul explained this in Galatians 2:20: "I have been crucified with Christ and I no longer live, but Christ lives in me. The life I live in the body, I live by faith in the Son of God, who loved me and gave himself for me."

Just as it's the water's job to hold us up in floating, it's Christ's job to live the Christian life through us. Our role is merely to surrender to Him and let Him live His life. This is the key to the Christian life.

This truth is so simple that most people ask, "What are *we* supposed to do if Christ does all the work?" The above verse says we are to live by faith. We are to trust Jesus to do exactly what He has promised to do: to live His life. That's all we *can* do. Jesus made that very clear when He said, "Apart from me you can do nothing" (John 15:5).

We have no other option in the Christian life than to trust Jesus Christ.

The Christian life is characterized by love, joy, peace, patience, kindness, goodness, faithfulness, gentleness, and self-control (Galatians 5:22,23). This is the fruit of the Spirit Christ produces in our lives.

It's impossible for us to produce the fruit of the Spirit through our own strength. As hard as we may try, love, joy, or peace won't be the final result of our efforts. Trying to produce these qualities is like trying to float. It doesn't work.

For example, have you ever *tried* to love an enemy or to experience the peace of God that passes understanding in the midst of rejection or a bad circumstance? How successful were you?

It's not hard to live the Christian life—it's *impossible!*

That's why our only option is to trust the One who can. And believe it or not, this is what pleases God. "Without faith it is impossible to please God" (Hebrews 11:6).

God never called us to "gut out" the Christian life. We can't live it even when we try. Recognize this fact and then make the intelligent decision to trust Jesus Christ. He's alive and has promised to live His life in and through you.

People at the beach would see my dad out in the water and say, "Look at that guy floating!" My dad took all the credit for floating, but he knew that he wasn't holding himself afloat. It was the water doing all the work. In the same way, people might think you're producing the Christian life. But if anything good is coming out of you, it's Christ who's doing the work. And believe me, no one will know that more than you will!

Are you tired of trying to live the Christian life? If so, are you willing to recognize that apart from Christ you can do nothing, and then trust Jesus Christ, the One who has promised to live the Christian life through you?

As you do this, you will begin to experience the abundant life that Jesus promised.

Chapter 41

The Pack and the Pickup

Cast all your anxiety on him because he cares for you.

1 Peter 5:7

DO YOU EVER HEAR CHRISTIANS talk about how hard it is to live the Christian life? The Christian life isn't *difficult* to live; it's *impossible*. However, most Christians try to live the Christian life through their own strength. They live as "practical atheists."

A practical atheist is someone who, when he encounters a problem in life, meets it as if he's the only resource available. This type of person reminds me of the story of the pickup truck and the hitchhiker.

A man is driving his pickup truck down the road when he sees a hitchhiker carrying a heavy load. He pulls over and offers a ride, which the hitchhiker gladly accepts.

A little way down the road, the driver looks in his rearview mirror and notices that the hitchhiker is hunched over in the bed of the truck, still carrying his heavy load over one shoulder. The driver stops and says, "Hey, buddy, why don't you put your pack down on the bed of the truck?"

"That's okay," responds the hitchhiker. "I don't want to bother you that much. Just take me to my destination, and I'll be happy."

How ridiculous! But this is the attitude of many Christians. They happily board the Lord's "salvation wagon" that will take them to heaven, but they shoulder the effort along the way.

What a contrast this attitude is to the words of Jesus: "Come to me, all you who are weary and burdened, and I will give you rest. Take my yoke upon you and learn from me, for I am gentle and humble in heart, and you will find rest for your souls. For my yoke is easy and my burden is light" (Matthew 11:28-30).

Jesus doesn't expect us to carry our own burdens in this life. As a matter of fact, Peter tells us, "Cast all your anxiety on him because he cares for you" (1 Peter 5:7). The Christian life is getting in the yoke with Jesus, allowing Him to carry our cares.

In other words, the Christian life is all up to Christ. Not only is He responsible for getting us to heaven, but He's also responsible for carrying us through this life on earth. And He's certainly big enough to handle any circumstance we may face.

Therefore we should live in total dependence upon Him in every area of life, trusting that He will cause "all things to work together for good" (Romans 8:28 NASB) and that His "grace is sufficient" (2 Corinthians 12:9) for any trial encountered in life.

You don't have to live as a practical atheist.

The Christian life begins in faith and is lived by faith in Jesus Christ. Make it your aim to experience the abundant life that Jesus has promised—through a life of total dependence upon Him and His love and grace.

Chapter 42

Mona Lisa

By one sacrifice he has made perfect forever those who are being made holy.

Hebrews 10:14

CHRISTIANS OFTEN MISPLACE THEIR dependence. One way we do this is by thinking it's our responsibility to make ourselves perfect. Too often we expect perfection of others and ourselves. When others or we don't match up to our expectations, we try to make improvements. Yet this is nothing more than trying to control our circumstances, which results in a life of total frustration.

The good news is the perfection we desire has been given to us by faith through Christ. We don't have to try to make ourselves perfect anymore. We are already perfect forever!

That's the message of Hebrews 10:14: "By one sacrifice he has made perfect forever those who are being made holy." Christ, by His sacrifice, can now present you holy in God's sight, without blemish, totally free from any accusation. When Jesus said upon the cross, "It is finished," He meant it! When something is finished, it's *complete*.

Let's suppose that during a trip to Paris I decide to tour the Louvre Museum. While walking through the galleries, I see Leonardo da Vinci's Mona Lisa. I'm so moved by this masterpiece that I buy it on the spot for millions and millions of dollars. I carefully ship it back home to my personal art studio.

As I look at the painting I start to think, "Maybe I can make this painting a little better." So I set it up on an easel, get out my paint, and begin dabbing on the Mona Lisa, trying to improve it. But there's no way that I can make this masterpiece better. The minute I add something of my own to da Vinci's work, I rob it of its value. The master's work is perfect as it is. There's nothing more I could do to improve the painting. Of course, the art world would think I had lost my mind if I attempted to do something like that.

In the same way, no one in his right mind would pull out a chisel to improve Michelangelo's David. No one would try to rewrite Beethoven's symphonies. These are the works of masters. They're meant to be enjoyed just as they are, and any effort on our part to improve on these would only cheapen the finished works of the masters.

But when it comes to the finished work of Jesus, so often we pull out our paints and try to improve on it. Yet there's nothing more we can add through our self-efforts to improve on what He has done.

He has already done it all.

Because of His sacrifice, we are perfect and complete forever.

Chapter 43

Reed and Marian

I am convinced that neither death nor life, neither angels nor demons, neither the present nor the future, nor any powers, neither height nor depth, nor anything else in all creation, will be able to separate us from the love of God that is in Christ Jesus our Lord.

Romans 8:38,39

THE GREATEST EXAMPLE I'VE WITNESSED of the peace of God transcending all understanding is the story of a young couple named Reed and Marian.

Reed was one of several fathers taking a girls' group on a camping trip to Oklahoma. Before leaving home in Dallas, the couple's 6-year-old daughter, Wendy, came up and asked, "Mommy, is it okay if I ride in the other car with my friend? She doesn't have anybody to ride with."

Marian said it was fine, and the group set out.

It was raining and the streets were slick. Before the group had gotten far, the driver of the car in which Wendy was riding lost control. He tried to bring the vehicle back into the lane, but the trailer they were hauling fishtailed. They crashed across the median and into the lane of oncoming traffic.

Miraculously, in a chain-reaction accident that eventually totaled 26 cars, the most serious injury was a broken arm to one of the girls—that is, except for Wendy.

Wendy was thrown out of the car and was killed instantly.

Just a few weeks later, one of Reed's closest friends died of cancer at the age of 32.

I was riding with Reed in a funeral limousine and noticed surprisingly that Reed was his usual soft-spoken, smiling self, even though his eyes were teary. In spite of everything, he seemed to be doing very well.

"Well, Reed," I said gently, "I suppose you've had enough of this to last you for a while."

He smiled and said, "That's for sure."

"Tell me," I asked. "How are you holding up? How have you learned to deal with the loss of Wendy?"

"Let me tell you about that," he said. "Marian and I look at it this way. What if God had come to us six years ago and made us an offer: 'Reed and Marian, I have a little girl, a daughter of Mine, named Wendy. She's only going to be on earth for six years. But I need someone who will love her, look after her, and teach her about Me for those six years. Then I'm going to take her home to Me. So I wonder: Would you like Me to give her to you, realizing that those are the conditions, or should I offer her to someone else?' Marian and I both would have said, 'Oh yes, Lord. Give her to us!' And that's just what we feel that God has done. He always knew that Wendy would only be on earth for six years. Marian and I have chosen to be thankful for every one of those six years that Wendy enriched our lives. We miss her terribly. We've cried, and we'll cry more tears. But we know that we'll see her again, and we thank God for it all."

What an attitude! In the face of great loss, Reed and Marian had thankful, not bitter hearts—thankful hearts that surrendered all their rights to a sovereign, loving God.

Because of their response of faith, that young couple has lived at peace ever since.

A tragedy? Yes! But Reed and Marian have discovered the reality of Romans 8:38,39:

> I am convinced that neither death nor life, neither angels nor demons, neither the present nor the future, nor any powers, neither height nor depth, nor anything else in all creation, will be able to separate us from the love of God that is in Christ Jesus our Lord.

But that's not the end of the story. Several years later the little girl Wendy had ridden with was reading my book *Classic Christianity,* and when she came to the story I've just related, she said to herself, "That was me in the car with Wendy!" That young lady wrote to me, telling me of the comfort she received from hearing Reed and Marian's story. She also told me she had shared the book with her dad, who had been living with years of guilt over the accident. When he read the story, this young woman said, a huge burden was lifted from her father's shoulders. She said knowing how Reed and Marian felt allowed her dad to open himself to the peace of God in a new and deeper way.

When tragedy occurs, as it surely will to all of us, can we purpose in our hearts to meet it with the same kind of utter dependence on the goodness of God that Reed and Marian displayed?

If we face each day with that attitude, we'll never know defeat or bitterness.

Chapter 44

The Light Bulb

A part from me you can do nothing.

John 15:5

WHY DOES A LIGHT BULB NEED electricity to function?

Because it's designed that way. If you separate the light bulb from the electricity, what do you have?

You've got a light bulb that can't behave like one. You might as well have a potato hanging out of the socket for all the light you're going to get out of it. That light bulb is a wonderful invention—very precisely designed. But it's designed so that it can't function apart from electricity.

Why does an oil lamp need oil to function?

It was made that way.

Why does a car need gasoline in it to function?

It too was made that way. Separate the car from the gas, and you've got a car on your hands that won't behave like one. You paid $20,000 for a car that won't run without some dollar-fifty gas in it.

Why does man need God in him in order to function?

He was made that way.

Separate God from man and what have you got? You've got a man all right, but he can't behave like one. He's not an animal so he can't behave like an animal, but he's not a true man as God made man to be, so he can't entirely behave like a man either. So he behaves like an idiot.

Salvation is getting God back into man, restoring him to his true humanity as God intended him to be. God *in the man* is indispensable to the true humanity of the man. Until you and I have God living in us, we're only two-thirds whole.

That's why we're always searching for something.

God intended us to live with our Creator inside His creation; and for us, the creation, to walk in dependence upon our Creator, not boss the Creator around.

So picture yourself as a light bulb. Are you connected to electricity—or are you sitting on the table, out of the socket—useless?

Part
Eight

TRUTH

Chapter 45

Follow Facts
Instead of Fantasy

Do not be anxious about anything, but in everything, by prayer and petition, with thanksgiving, present your requests to God. And the peace of God, which transcends all understanding, will guard your hearts and your minds in Christ Jesus.

Philippians 4:6,7

WE'VE ALL HEARD THE SAYING "If it feels good, do it!"

This modern-day philosophy makes our feelings or emotions the criteria for truth. Truth, however, isn't and can't be determined by feelings.

God has so engineered man that our emotions are merely responders to what we're thinking. Proverbs 23:7 (NASB) puts it this way: "As [a man] thinks within himself, so he is."

It's always been that way, and as long as we function in a body of flesh on this earth, it always will be. Whatever I'm thinking will determine the way I feel. Emotions always follow thought. That's the way we've been designed by God.

Emotions have no ability to think on their own. They can't reason. They can't discern the past from the future or the future from the present. Neither can they discern truth from error. They always predictably *respond* to what we allow into our minds through our "eye gates" or our "ear gates"; or to our thinking patterns, whether proper or improper.

Most of you have been to a scary movie at one time or another. There were probably dozens of other people in the theater with you, and before you sat down you knew that you would be seeing a staged event. It wouldn't be real—only images created by light projected through a long strip of film. Yet when "Jaws" jumped out of that water, your heart practically leaped out of your chest. Whether you're a man or woman, it mattered little at that point as you shrieked at the top of your lungs (or wanted to)!

Emotions are like that. They can't discern the real from the imaginary. They didn't know that what you were seeing on the screen was fiction. Therefore they predictably responded to what came into your mind through your eyes and your ears.

When I was younger, I went with my brother and sister to see what was (up to that time) one of the most horrifying motion pictures ever produced. Intellectually, I knew it wasn't real, but when Norman Bates tore into that shower in *Psycho*, I crawled under my seat in sheer terror! I practically embarrassed my brother and sister to death.

Why did I react that way? My emotions didn't know that I wasn't in that shower in *Psycho*. They couldn't tell fact from fiction and began to run wild.

Our emotional state will always be related directly to what we're thinking. We can't subject our eyes and ears to scenes of horror and experience peaceful serenity at the same time. We can't dwell on angry thoughts and at the same time experience joy in our hearts. We can't dwell on sad thoughts without being overtaken by sadness. Nor can we dwell on depressing thoughts and not expect to ultimately become depressed.

God gave us a mind, and what we allow to come into it will dictate our emotional responses. Whether what we see and hear is fact or fantasy, whether what we're considering is truth or error, whether we're contemplating the past, future, or present, our emotions will respond to what we're thinking. They have no choice.

Typically the way we operate is that we think something, then feel something, and then do something. Our actions are a direct result of what we're feeling. If we're to experience freedom in our lives, however, we must let truth, not our feelings, determine our actions.

From God's vantage point, the way we should operate is first to think something, then act on it by faith —and then we can experience the emotions God wants us to experience.

Philippians 4:6,7 is our model in this:

> Do not be anxious about anything, but in everything, by prayer and petition, with thanksgiving, present your requests to God. And the peace of God, which transcends all understanding, will guard your hearts and your minds in Christ Jesus.

It says we're not to be anxious about anything. Now what is anxiety? It's an emotion. You say, "Okay, Lord, what do You want me to do?" He tells you to present your requests to Him with an attitude of thanksgiving. He's the only One who can take care of the circumstances you're anxious about. Therefore this verse says to trust Him. And what happens?

When you act upon this truth by faith, you'll experience the peace of God that passes understanding. The truth of God comes into your mind, you act upon it by faith, and then you experience peace.

The battleground for your emotions begins in the mind. If your emotions are out of control, it's not because you have emotional problems. You have *thinking* problems.

The solution is to begin renewing your mind with truth and then acting on this truth by faith, regardless of what your emotions may be telling you to do. Romans 12:2 gives us the pattern:

> Do not conform any longer to the pattern of this world, but be transformed by the renewing of your mind. Then you will be able to test and approve what God's will is— his good, pleasing and perfect will.

If you're in bondage to your emotions, recognize that your emotions are predictably responding to what you're thinking.

Let God renew your mind with truth. Then you'll be able to experience the peace of God that passes understanding and enjoy the freedom that is yours in Christ.

Chapter 46

The Teddy Bear
and the Puppy

Live by the Spirit, and you will not gratify the desires of the flesh. For the flesh desires what is contrary to the Spirit, and the Spirit what is contrary to the flesh. They are in conflict with each other, so that you do not do what you want.

Galatians 5:16,17

HAVE YOU EVER FOUND YOURSELF ASKING, "Why do I keep doing that?"

All of us at some time or another have struggled with bad habits. The frustrating thing is the more we try to overcome these bad habits, the more we find ourselves doing them.

What we fail to understand is that when we become preoccupied with self and focus on our shortcomings, the inevitable result is failure. When we're busy trying to clean up the flesh, where's the focus of our minds? On cleaning up the flesh. "Whatever a man sows, this he will also reap. For the one who

175

sows to his own flesh shall from the flesh reap corruption" (Galatians 6:7,8 NASB). To free ourselves from bad habits, we must take our focus off ourselves.

In Romans 7:18, Paul states flatly, "I know that nothing good lives in me, that is, in my flesh." And in the fifty-third chapter of Isaiah the prophet declares, "We all, like sheep, have gone astray, each of us has turned to his own way" (verse 6).

The truth is this: As long as we live in a body of flesh, sin will indwell us. How then can we purify ourselves of the very thing that indwells us?

In and of ourselves, it's impossible. Therefore, the most sensible thing we can do is heed the instruction of Paul in Romans 6:11: "Count yourselves dead to sin but alive to God in Christ Jesus." The question then becomes, "But how do I accomplish this?"

In Galatians 5:16 (NASB) Paul provides the answer: "Walk by the Spirit, and you will not carry out the desire of the flesh." Notice that he didn't say that the desires of the flesh would go away. Nor did he say to clean up the flesh so you can walk in the Spirit. Not fulfilling the desires of the flesh is a *result* of walking in the Spirit.

It's like a baby in a playpen, focusing his attention on his favorite stuffed animal: a teddy bear. He holds on to that bear for dear life, and if anyone tries to take it away, that baby screams at the top of his lungs! He's focused on that bear which is his security blanket, and no one is going to take it away. It's soft and cuddly. It looks back at him. And it's always there, waiting for a hug.

How in the world can we ever shift this child's dependence off the teddy bear?

Easy. Get him a puppy. Just drop a puppy in the playpen and watch what happens. This puppy is warm. It wiggles, moves around, makes sounds, and wags its tail 90 miles an hour. When the baby pets it, the puppy licks him back—even seems to like him. Why, this is great! Who needs that dumb bear anymore? This puppy is alive! It's a lot more fun than a stuffed animal.

Once the child has become preoccupied with the puppy, all you need to do is reach into the playpen and take the teddy bear out. The baby won't even realize it's gone.

So it is with bad habits. Fall in love with Jesus, get preoccupied with His life, then you'll see the bad habits simply falling away. If you want to let go of a bad habit, then get your eyes on Jesus. It's not enough to tell people what they should stop doing. They must develop a totally new mind-set—a new preoccupation. We're not able to let go of things until we have something new to hang on to.

Are there bad habits in your life that you've been trying to get rid of?

If so, forget about the habit and focus your attention on Christ. Soon you'll experience what Paul described in Galatians 5:16 (NASB):

Walk by the Spirit, and you will not carry out the desire of the flesh.

Chapter 47

The AM-FM Radio

Do not conform any longer to the pattern of this world, but be transformed by the renewing of your mind. Then you will be able to test and approve what God's will is—his good, pleasing and perfect will.

Romans 12:2

WITHIN EVERY CHRISTIAN ARE BOTH the desires of the flesh and the desires of the Spirit. Paul tells us in Galatians 5:17 that these desires are in conflict one with another. We all know this to be true. If someone insults us, our flesh wants to get back at that person, even though the Spirit of God living inside says to forgive. Which desire do we follow? This is a battle that every Christian encounters, and this battle begins in the mind.

Our mind functions in a way that can be compared to an AM-FM radio. An AM-FM radio has been designed to receive both AM and FM signals. The AM signal carries programming that can only be heard on the AM dial; and the FM signal carries programming that can only be heard on the FM dial. A radio listener doesn't have a choice as to the programming on either signal. He does have a choice, however, as to which signal, AM or FM, he will listen to.

So it is with our minds.

We've been created in such a way that our minds can receive input from Satan and the world and from God and His Word. The programming on the AM dial of our mind comes from Satan and the world. Satan and the world fill our minds with lies or error that appeal to the flesh and its desires.

> Everything in the world—the cravings of sinful man, the lust of his eyes and the boasting of what he has and does—comes not from the Father but from the world (1 John 2:16).

The programming on the FM dial of our minds comes from God and His Word. This is *truth* that appeals to the Spirit and its desires.

> As it is written: "No eye has seen, no ear has heard, no mind has conceived what God has prepared for those who love him"—but God has revealed it to us by his Spirit....We have not received the spirit of the world but the Spirit who is from God, that we may understand what God has freely given us (1 Corinthians 2:9,10,12).

Just like the radio, we can't change the programming that comes from Satan, nor can we change the programming that comes from God. However, we can choose whether we will listen to Satan and his error or God and His truth.

Jesus said in John 8:31,32: "If you hold to my teaching, you are really my disciples. Then you will know the truth, and the truth will set you free." If truth sets you free, then error must put you in bondage. If you choose to listen to Satan and the world, you'll experience bondage. If you choose to listen to God and His Word, you'll experience freedom.

The error that comes from Satan says:

- worry about everything
- you have to be a lot better than *that* to please God
- analyze yourself to see why you're so bad
- you deserve to be treated better than that
- you won't be happy until you get _____
- blame people for your problems
- wonder what tomorrow will bring

On the other hand, truth that comes from God answers all these errors:

- "Be anxious for nothing" (Philippians 4:6 NASB).
- "By one sacrifice he has made [you] perfect forever" (Hebrews 10:14).
- "Consider yourselves to be dead to sin, but alive to God" (Romans 6:11 NASB).
- Love "does not take into account a wrong suffered" (1 Corinthians 13:5 NASB).
- "I have learned to be content whatever the circumstances" (Philippians 4:11).
- "Take the log out of your own eye" (Matthew 7:5 NASB).
- "Do not be anxious for tomorrow; for tomorrow will care for itself" (Matthew 6:34 NASB).

For a Christian, who to listen to seems like an easy choice. Who in their right mind would choose bondage over freedom?

We do, however. Why? Because our emotions respond to whatever is in our minds. Satan gets his programming into our minds through our five senses. And what we see, hear, feel, taste, or smell produces an emotional response. It's through this emotional response that the desires of the flesh are cultivated. At this point, because we're so feelings-oriented, it becomes very easy to act out the desires of the flesh.

Truth, however, isn't determined by feelings. Just because we feel something doesn't mean it's true. We are therefore not to let feelings dictate what our actions will be. That's why the Bible tells us not to conform any longer "to the pattern of this world, but be transformed by the renewing of your mind. Then you will be able to test and approve what God's will is—his good, pleasing and perfect will" (Romans 12:2).

Jesus Christ lives inside each believer and is constantly feeding truth into our minds in every circumstance we encounter. Jesus Christ is there to remind us of our identity in Him, of His constant love and forgiveness, and of the sufficiency of His grace. Based on the truth of His love and grace, He reasons with us and then asks us to present our bodies to Him regardless of what our emotions are telling us to do.

> I urge you, brothers, in view of God's mercy, to offer your bodies as living sacrifices, holy and pleasing to God—this is your spiritual act of worship (Romans 12:1).

> Do not offer the parts of your body to sin, as instruments of wickedness, but rather offer yourselves to God, as those who have been brought from death to life; and offer the parts of your body to him as instruments of righteousness (Romans 6:13).

When we do, we'll be able to test and approve God's will—His good, pleasing, and perfect will.

Whether you experience bondage or the freedom which is God's will is determined by whether you listen to Satan and his error or to God and His truth.

To which dial will you tune your mind?

Chapter 48

Snapping and Tapping

*I*t is God who works in you to will and to act
according to his good purpose.

Philippians 2:13

IS YOUR CHRISTIAN LIFE GENUINE, authentic, real? Or are you
merely going through the motions, imitating what you see in
others? Consider this scenario:

A gentleman is sitting in a room with headphones on, listening to music. The music is lively, and soon he's snapping his
fingers and tapping his toes to the rhythm.

Soon a deaf man enters the room. He immediately sees the
first man and walks over to him and smiles a greeting. For a few
minutes the deaf man watches the music-lover, who's obviously

enjoying himself, and whose whole body wants to respond to what his ears are receiving.

"He sure seems to be enjoying himself," the deaf man thinks. "I think I'll try it, too."

So the deaf man sits next to the first man and begins to imitate him. Awkwardly and haltingly at first, he tries to snap his fingers, tap his toes, and move like the person next to him. Everybody has some sense of rhythm, whether they can hear or not.

After a little practice the deaf man is snapping and tapping in time with the first man. He even smiles a little and shrugs: "It's not that much fun," he thinks, "but it's okay."

Then a third man walks into the room. What does he see? Two men apparently doing the same thing. But is there a difference?

Absolutely! All the difference in the world! The first man's actions are natural responses to the music he hears. The deaf man is only imitating those outward actions—and he can't hear a note of the music.

That's the difference between real Christianity and legalism, between living our lives based on truth versus living our lives based on error.

That's the way it is for many so-called Christians. They know that the Christian life is an abundant life—they see it in some of their friends. So they try to imitate the things their friends do. They may join a church, read the Bible, pray, and engage in all sorts of "religious" activities.

But they're not happy. Why not?

Because their life isn't based on truth. They aren't plugged into the music, so their only hope is to imitate what others are doing. Even though their actions may look similar to those of the abundant life, they aren't experiencing the real thing.

When we approach the Christian life in the way God intended, our attitudes and actions are a response to the "music" we hear. That music is our personal relationship with the living Christ who indwells us. It's the music of walking in a trust relationship with a loving God and Father whom we're learning to love more and more every day.

On the other hand, a legalist doesn't hear the music. All legalism cares about is getting people to tap and snap at the right time! The legalist will always say that an emphasis on grace will lead to more sinning. But that's not what the Bible says!

> The grace of God that brings salvation has appeared to all men. It [the grace of God!] teaches us to say "No" to ungodliness and worldly passions, and to live self-controlled, upright and godly lives in this present age, while we wait for the blessed hope—the glorious appearing of our great God and Savior, Jesus Christ (Titus 2:11-13).

The grace and love of God is the true motivation for the Christian life according to the Bible. That's the real music that should be the source of our lives.

The error of trying to clean ourselves up by adhering to legalistic standards is like saying, "If you'll tap and snap correctly, you'll hear the music."

No! God wants us to listen to His music—the message of His unconditional love and acceptance—and then respond to what we hear!

Chapter 49

The Way and the Life Bookends

I am the way and the truth and the life. No one comes to the Father except through me.

John 14:6

IT'S INTERESTING HOW MODERN Christianity interprets this verse. Everyone certainly agrees that Jesus is the only way to the Father, and anyone who says there are other ways to God we would label as a heretic.

The same is true concerning life. We all agree there's no other life available than that which is given to us by Jesus Christ. Buddha can't give life, Muhammad can't give life, and obedience to the law can't give life. There's only one life and that's the Lord Jesus Christ. Again, anyone who would disagree we would label as a heretic. However, when it comes to the truth, we have a different mind-set altogether.

It's much like a bookshelf. On the bookshelf sit two book-ends labeled "The Way" and "The Life." In between we tend to see numerous books on truth. There's psychological truth, there's scientific truth, there's philosophical truth, and there's biblical truth.

As we operate under the premise that all truth is God's truth, we try to combine a little psychological truth, a little biblical truth, a little philosophical truth, and come up with a nice blend—because we're not firmly rooted in Christ's words that *He* is the truth. We readily accept what the psychological world, philosophical world, or scientific world tells us is true.

For example, we see Christians coming up with theories and explanations that combine the creation story and evolutionists' views to explain the origins of this earth and of mankind.

We also see the church lapping up psychological theory like a cat lapping up milk, and we wonder why the church is in the shape it's in today.

Jesus is the Way, the Truth, and the Life. Just as we hold dogmatically to the fact that He is the Way and the Life, let's also hold dogmatically to the fact that He is the Truth.

In so doing, we'll avoid a lot of heartbreak that results from accepting other sources of "truth," which in fact are simply error dressed up to look like truth.

Chapter 50

Sanctification

*I*t is God's will that you should be sanctified.

1 Thessalonians 4:3

*S*anctify them by the truth; your word is truth.

John 17:17

THE WORD SANCTIFIED COMES FROM the same root word as "holy." It means to be "set apart." It's not—as we often think—full of negative connotations, such as, "I'm sanctified and that means I've got my Bible under my arm and I walk with my head tilted to one side and kind of grin and act real holy with people."

That's not what sanctified means at all. It's an extremely practical word. Sanctification means to be set apart for the specific purpose for which something is created.

For example, if you're wearing shoes today, you're "sanctifying" your shoes. You're using shoes for the purpose for which they were created. Shoes were made for your feet. If you've got them on your feet, you're sanctifying your shoes. If you were to hang them on your ear as a new kind of earring, you wouldn't be sanctifying them.

If you wear eyeglasses, you're sanctifying them as you wear them. You're using them for the purpose for which they were created. They were created to help you see. You've got them on—you're seeing better—you're sanctifying your glasses. If you stir your coffee with them, you're not sanctifying your glasses.

If you're wearing a watch and you glance at the time, in so doing you're sanctifying your watch. If you use your watch to crack peanuts, you're not sanctifying your watch.

When you're sanctified by faith, it means that as a person who has exercised faith in Jesus, you've been set apart from the entire world that does not believe in Jesus. It doesn't mean that you wear your hair in a bun. It means that you've been set apart by God because of your relationship with Jesus. It means you've been set apart for the intelligent purpose for which you were created—to be available to the living God for Him to live His life through you. And yet because we don't believe that God has done His work completely, we continue to try to progressively sanctify ourselves by the way we dress, by the way we act, and by the way we speak.

We make ourselves obnoxious by trying to improve upon what Jesus has already accomplished. The very moment you stepped out of Adam and into Christ, and Christ stepped out of heaven and into you, you were set apart, sanctified, from the rest of the world.

So don't be afraid of the word sanctification. It's a wonderful word that confirms you're being used for the exact purpose for which you were created.

It gave me great joy to have some brothers come and tell about your faithfulness to the truth and how you continue to walk in the truth.

3 John 3

TRUTH MATTERS MORE than sincerity.

When I was in high school, I was hired one summer as a farm worker. I'm sure this doesn't sound too thrilling, but back then I was extremely excited to have a real paying job.

Just as a beautiful dawn was breaking on our first day out, I piled onto the back of a truck with several other temporary workers and was driven out to the fields. Our assignment was to hoe the tomato section. Our supervisor took a hoe and very carefully explained what we were to do. Certain weeds tended to grow around the tomato plants, so we were to go down the rows with our tools, clearing away the weeds.

My father had always impressed upon me the importance and value of hard work, so I attacked my new job with a vengeance. I was determined to be the best worker they had. I worked hard all morning, pushing myself to continue through the fatigue. And so it was with a sense of great satisfaction, as well as several new aches and blisters, that I sat down under a shade tree for our lunch break.

I hadn't sat there five minutes before I heard a bloodcurdling scream, followed by a long stream of obscenities. We all knew that someone was in trouble and turned to see what would happen.

"Some idiot hoed down a whole section of tomato plants and left the weeds!" the supervisor screamed.

Like the others, I looked around, wondering what moron he could have been talking about. After questioning a few people, the supervisor discovered who had done it.

It was me!

I can honestly say that I had been working in total sincerity—and working *hard*—trying to give my boss a full return for my wages. Instead, I had done more damage than good.

Sincerity is a wonderful thing, but this very embarrassing incident illustrates an important truth: You can be totally sincere but be sincerely wrong. This has direct application to the process of growing in grace.

I am reminded of this story when I hear Christians speak in glowing terms of the qualities of self-discipline and dedication. Those are qualities that we seem to instinctively admire in a person. But self-discipline and dedication *in and of themselves* aren't necessarily good things.

We need to ask—are these qualities being directed *toward the proper goal?* A person may be sincerely disciplined and dedicated but be applying himself in the wrong direction, just as I did in the tomato patch. He can be directing these qualities to the attainment of a meaningless or even harmful end.

The Nazis are an extreme example of such misdirected dedication. They were highly motivated and supremely self-controlled, but these qualities were dedicated toward evil ends.

The same holds true of the Pharisees in Jesus' time. They were possibly the ultimate in religious dedication, yet Christ called them hypocrites, blind guides, whitewashed tombs, snakes, and a brood of vipers (Matthew 23:13,16,27,33).

No doubt the Galatians were totally sincere in their efforts to perfect themselves through obedience to the law of Moses, but Paul had no words of praise for their dedication to self-improvement:

> You foolish Galatians! Who has bewitched you? Before your very eyes Jesus Christ was clearly portrayed as crucified. I would like to learn just one thing from you: Did you receive the Spirit by observing the law, or by believing what you heard? Are you so foolish? After beginning with the Spirit, are you now trying to attain your goal by human effort? (Galatians 3:1-3).

Paul would undoubtedly experience the same turmoil of spirit were he to come back and witness the state of Christianity today. Just like the Galatians, millions of Christians have trusted in Christ for their eternal destiny and entrance into heaven but are trying to live out their Christian lives through dependence on self-effort. Having forgotten, or never having learned, the truth that Jesus taught—"apart from me you can do nothing"—they are applying tremendous energy and concentration to produce what only Christ can produce, with disastrous results.

In the same way I worked with my hoe, they are working feverishly—enduring blisters, sweat, and tears—to produce what God does not want.

And yet the very fruit they seek through their self-efforts are available freely through Christ. Love, joy, peace, patience—all the fruit of the Spirit are just that—*fruit*. Trying to work at producing Christian fruit is like tying oranges on an apple tree and calling it an orange tree. The result is error, not truth.

The fruit must grow based on the life within. Apple trees can only produce apples. And self-effort, no matter how sincerely motivated, can never produce the fruit that only comes from the Spirit of God living inside a person.

Part Nine

FREEDOM

Chapter 52

The Cafeteria

Sin shall not be your master, because you are not under law, but under grace. What then? Shall we sin because we are not under law but under grace? By no means!

Romans 6:14,15

WHENEVER THE PURE MESSAGE OF God's love and acceptance in Jesus Christ is taught, an objection is always raised: "You're giving people a license to sin."

This objection isn't new. In fact, Paul asked and answered this objection in his letter to the Romans. "What shall we say, then? Shall we go on sinning so that grace may increase?... What then? Shall we sin because we are not under law but under grace?" (Romans 6:1,15).

To both questions Paul's answer is "By no means!" It's as if he were saying, "What an absurd question!" And it *is* an absurd question when you understand the love and grace of God and know that Christ lives in you.

Imagine that you own a fine cafeteria. One day you hear a tremendous commotion in the alley where the garbage dumpsters are. There you find the most pitiful-looking human being you've ever seen fighting with several stray cats over the food scraps in the dumpster.

Moved with compassion, you approach the guy and say, "Listen, I can't stand to see you eating garbage. Come into my cafeteria and eat."

"I don't have any money," he replies.

"It doesn't matter," you respond. "You can eat at my cafeteria every day absolutely free of charge."

Taking the guy by the arm, you lead him inside. There in front of him are vegetables...salads...fruits...beef...fish...chicken...cakes...pies.

"Eat anything you want," you say. "It's yours for the taking."

With unbelieving eyes he asks, "Do you really mean that I can eat anything I want?"

"Yes, you may eat anything you want."

Standing in front of the most fabulous spread of food he could imagine, with the offer to eat anything for free, what if the guy looked at you and asked, "Can I go back to the dumpster and eat more garbage?"

You'd think the guy was crazy. In the face of all that delicious food, all he can think to ask is whether he can eat garbage. How ridiculous!

Jesus Christ laid down His life for us to take away our sins and to free us from the bondage of sin and death. Then, raised from the dead, Jesus gave us His very life to experience: a life characterized by love, joy, peace, patience, kindness, goodness, faithfulness, gentleness, and self-control.

And in the face of a "cafeteria line" like this, that Jesus called "abundant" life (John 10:10), all some of us can think to ask is, "Does that mean I can go out and sin more?" In other words, "Can I continue eating garbage?"

Somehow we've missed the goal of the Christian life.

Instead we're still obsessed with sin. Most of our preaching and teaching is directed toward getting people to quit sinning. In our analogy, instead of saying to the starving man, "Come and eat," most Christian teaching would say, "Stay out of the garbage! Don't eat the garbage!" It's no wonder we're more interested in garbage than we are in cafeteria food.

First Corinthians 15:56 says, "The sting of death is sin, and the power of sin is the law." Like the garbage, sin looks pretty good when you constantly hear, "Don't sin. You have to quit sinning." That's why the goal of the Christian life isn't to quit sinning. Jesus didn't come so that we would quit sinning. He came that we might "have life, and have it to the full" (John 10:10).

Garbage will lose its appeal to our starving man once he gets into the cafeteria line and begins experiencing what good food tastes like. In the same way, sin loses its appeal once a person begins to experience the very life of Christ. The life of Christ is what every human being needs. We need to experience daily the reality of knowing Christ and walking with Him in a vibrant relationship.

The Lord defined eternal life this way: "This is eternal life: that they may know you, the only true God, and Jesus Christ, whom you have sent" (John 17:3). That's the real goal of the Christian life: knowing Christ!

It's only in comparison with the riches of knowing Christ that sin begins to lose its appeal. As a matter of fact, sin becomes stupid. It's so dumb to settle for anything less than experiencing

Jesus Christ Himself. Why should you ever wallow in the garbage when the Lord has provided a banquet table?

No, the grace of God does not give us a license to sin. The grace of God frees us from the bondage of sin and death and allows us to experience the very life of Christ. We are beloved, accepted children of God, who have been called to His banquet table to experience Jesus Christ living in and through us every day.

Abundant life isn't "pie in the sky." It's real, and it's ours for the taking if we'll only believe.

Let's not settle for anything less!

Chapter 53

Weeding the Lawn

*L*ive by the Spirit, and you will not gratify the desires of the flesh. For the flesh desires what is contrary to the Spirit, and the Spirit what is contrary to the flesh. They are in conflict with each other, so that you do not do what you want.

Galatians 5:16,17

WHEN I LIVED IN CALIFORNIA, we used to have to weed our lawn frequently. We'd get out there, and we'd pull them and pull them. And if you didn't get them by the root, they'd grow back. Sometimes it seemed like they grew back anyway. And it's funny how the weeds seem to grow so much faster than the plants you really want in your yard.

If you want to maintain a good yard or garden, how long will you have to pull weeds? Will one weeding a season do the trick? No! You're going to have to plan on pulling weeds for the rest of your life.

I was getting pretty tired of continually weeding, and one day a neighbor came along, looked at my lawn and said, "Bob, why don't you grow some good grass—that'll take care of those weeds."

And he was right. Here's what happens when you grow good grass—it chokes out the weeds. They die off, replaced by the lush green grass.

In the spiritual life, this preoccupation with weeds is desert religion—it's a continual preoccupation with sin—and it's a backbreaking, never-ending job. But to be preoccupied with growing good grass is like walking in grace and freedom.

The goal of the Christian life is not to pull weeds—to stop sinning. God calls us to walk by faith in Him. As we do, the result is that we will not fulfill the desires of the flesh. The weeds are crowded out!

So what do you want to do, pull weeds the rest of your life—or grow grass? To be in bondage—or to walk in freedom?

Chapter 54

Monkeying Around

To the Jews who had believed him, Jesus said, "If you hold to my teaching, you are really my disciples. Then you will know the truth, and the truth will set you free."

John 8:31,32

MUCH OF THE CHRISTIAN WORLD lives in spiritual bondage today. The reason is we hold to unscriptural misconceptions of what the Christian life is all about. Our misconceptions range from our understanding of forgiveness and identity in Christ to how we're supposed to live the Christian life every day.

The way that we hold to these misconceptions and remain in spiritual bondage reminds me of how monkeys are captured in the tropics. The natives hollow out a coconut, fill the coconut with sweet beans, and then attach it to the base of a tree.

After dark, the monkey comes by and notices the sweet beans in the coconut. He reaches in through the hole in the coconut and takes hold of the beans. In grabbing the beans, the monkey makes a fist that's too large to remove. He won't let go of the beans, and he can't take his hand out of the coconut. So the monkey just sits there. The next morning the natives come by and pick the dumb thing up still holding onto his beans.

All the monkey had to do to go free was let go of the sweet beans. And so it is with us. All we have to do to go free in our Christian experience is let go of the misconceptions we're grasping concerning the Christian life.

This is the point Jesus was making to His hearers when He said, "If you hold to my teaching, you are really my disciples. Then you will know the truth, and the truth will set you free" (John 8:31,32).

Several years ago, when I was involved in the busiest Christian schedule you could imagine and experiencing burnout, that verse came to mind. I was busy doing things for the Lord, but I was barren and didn't know why. My Christian life felt more like a job than a relationship with the living God. It suddenly occurred to me that if truth sets you free, the opposite had to be true—error puts you in bondage. I knew that I wasn't free, and there was only one reason why: I must be living according to error rather than according to truth.

Once I realized truth sets you free and error binds you, my next thought was to ask, "What error have I grabbed hold of concerning the Christian life?" As I've said, my life was busy and barren. I used to tell people that "Christianity isn't a religion; it's a relationship with God through His Son, Jesus Christ." The joy of my salvation left because I had strayed from my relationship with God back to practicing a religion. That was the error I was grasping.

What was the solution?

Just like the monkey, all I had to do was to let go of the error and start believing truth. I asked the Lord to teach me the truth He promised would set me free. And that's what He did. He showed me afresh that Christianity isn't a religion. It's a relationship. John describes it this way: "This is eternal life: that they may know you, the only true God, and Jesus Christ, whom you have sent" (John 17:3).

Today my relationship with God is even more exciting than when it first began.

What about your relationship with Christ? Are you in bondage today?

If so, it's because you're holding on to error concerning the Christian life.

Nothing good can come from holding onto something that is keeping you from experiencing the abundance of life that God has promised, and experiencing day by day the freedom that is found only in Christ Jesus our Lord.

Are you willing to let go and let God teach you the truth that will set you free?

Chapter 55

Amy's Story

*O*ur *citizenship is in heaven. And we eagerly await a Savior from there, the Lord Jesus Christ.*

Philippians 3:20

MY WIFE, AMY, WAS BORN IN RUSSIA and lived in Germany after the war. While in the army, I married her and brought her to the United States.

As an American citizen today, she has no relation whatsoever to the Communist doctrine she heard as a child. She has full citizenship in a different country, a free country. She has a new identity as an American.

Let's say, though, some Russian agents were following her around, saying, "You're Russian. You have to do what we tell you. You can't change who you are. You work for us."

There's no reason to waste time arguing with them. Amy could just rely on the truth and say, "Get lost. I don't have any relation to you anymore. I am free from the bondage of my past. My identity is no longer Russian. I am an American citizen! I'm subject to the rights, privileges, and laws of the United States of America. I am *free*. Now, get out of here, or I'll call the police!"

That's how we're to deal with the lies of the devil.

We all know the experience of wanting to be everything God wants us to be and yet failing. We know the whispering voice in our ear:

"You'll never make it. You're a miserable Christian. God has forsaken you. You're totally unacceptable."

When you hear false accusations like these, don't waste time and effort arguing with the devil. Just reject the lie and fall back on who God says you are!

Assert boldly, "I am a child of God. If you don't like something about me, Satan, take it up with Jesus. He's my Lord. I have no relation to you at all."

Amy can say, "I am dead to Russia, and alive to the United States." In the same way, we can say, "I am dead to sin and to the wages of it and alive to God."

Romans 6:3,4 (NASB) says:

> Do you not know that all of us who have been baptized into Christ Jesus have been baptized into His death? Therefore we have been buried with Him through baptism into death, in order that as Christ was raised from the dead through the glory of the Father, so we too might walk in newness of life.

Because we've experienced God's "great exchange," we can consider the past dead and gone—and concentrate on walking in the new life we have received.

Remember that you're not a citizen of Satan's domain anymore. You now belong to God's kingdom and all the rights of first-class citizenship are yours.

Chapter 56

Slavery

It is for freedom that Christ has set us free. Stand firm, then, and do not let yourselves be burdened again by a yoke of slavery.

Galatians 5:1

NOT TOO MANY YEARS AGO slavery was widely practiced in this country. It was one of the most ungodly atrocities that has ever befallen America.

Envision for a moment standing at a slave market, and here is a huge hulk of a man, in chains, to be auctioned off as a human slave, a piece of chattel.

The auction starts.

"Who'll give me ten dollars?" the auctioneer calls.

And the bidders respond with enthusiasm.

Soon the auctioneer is fielding bids of one hundred dollars, then two hundred for the man. The price goes up to a point where nobody can bid except one man who's extremely wealthy. And he offers top dollar.

The auctioneer says "Sold!" The transaction is complete.

The slave is brought down to his new owner. The owner is given the key to the man's chains. He then reaches down and unlocks the chains and removes them from the man.

He looks at the man he just bought and says, "Sir, go free."

The slave looks at him and says, "Sir, I thought you bought me."

The wealthy man says, "I did. I bought you to set you free. Now go free."

The man says, "I don't understand. Why are you doing this?"

"Because I love you. And because God didn't create you to be a slave. He created you to be free."

At this the slave asks, "Sir, where do you live?"

"Oh, I live just over the hill there," answers the wealthy man.

"Where are you going now?" asks the now–former slave.

"I'm going home."

"Sir, can I go with you?"

"Sure. But only if you want to—not because you have to. But if you want to go with me, I'd love to have you come and be my friend."

The slave looks the man in the eye and says without reservation, "When a man loves me like that, I want to go home with him forever."

That man was purchased so that he could be set free.

Folks, I believe some of the deepest knowledge of God was experienced over and over during that awful era of slavery. The slaves had nothing. They were stripped of everything.

All they had was Jesus. And by having Him, they had everything.

Many beautiful and meaningful songs came out of slavery. They're songs of a deep understanding of Jesus. Back in those days, one of the ways they kept slavery going was by prohibiting the slaves from having shoes. That way, if they ever escaped, they'd be easier to find barefooted. People would easily spot them as slaves and turn them in.

Those slaves didn't have shoes or freedom, but they knew that someday they would have shoes and *would* be free. And that's how the great spiritual was born, "I got shoes, you got shoes, all God's children got shoes. And when I get to heaven I'm gonna put on my shoes, gonna dance all over God's heaven, heaven—gonna dance all over God's heaven."

Why'd they sing that?

Because they knew someday they were going to be in the presence of Jesus, and they were going to have their shoes in heaven.

The Lord Jesus Christ has set you and me free—because He bought us so He could set us free.

Don't let yourself be yoked again to this burden of slavery.

Don't let anyone ever put you back under the law again.

But go *free* in Jesus Christ!

Chapter 57

The Phantom Christian

Accept one another, then, just as Christ accepted you, in order to bring praise to God.

Romans 15:7

MOST CHRISTIANS CAN EASILY QUOTE John 3:16: "For God so loved the world...." Nonetheless, many Christians walk around every day feeling that God is sick to His stomach because of their failure to live up to His standards.

Often though, it's not even God's standards Christians are trying to keep, but regulations imposed by themselves or other people. They're trying to be what I like to call the "Phantom Christian."

The Phantom Christian is that imaginary person to whom many of us are continually comparing ourselves. He's the superspiritual man who gets up every day at 4:00 A.M. to pray for several hours. Then he reads 30 chapters in his Bible. He goes to work (at which he is tops in his field), where he effectively shares Christ with everyone in his office. He teaches several Bible studies, goes to church every time the doors are open, and serves on several committees. He's also a wonderful spiritual leader at home—a sterling example of a loving husband and father, who leads stimulating family devotions every day for his "Proverbs 31 wife" and perfect children.

Of course no one could live up to such a standard. Even if some person had the ability, he would still need a hundred hours in a day to perform like this Phantom Christian!

Rationally, we all know the idea of the Phantom Christian is ridiculous, but somehow he remains in the back of our minds, creating in us a sense of failure to measure up. That's why many, many Christians live under continual guilt. To those who believe that the Phantom Christian is God's standard for acceptance, God seems a million miles away, sitting in heaven with His arms folded in disapproval.

People in this bondage know well the biblical teaching that God loves them, but they clearly don't believe in their hearts that God *accepts* them. And apart from knowing about and resting in God's acceptance, His love becomes practically meaningless and irrelevant in daily living.

I've often talked of God's love in counseling appointments and seen Christians react bitterly to the words.

"So what?" they say. "He loves everybody!"

Apart from acceptance, God's love becomes vague, universal, impersonal.

But this vitally-needed acceptance by God certainly isn't earned by the Phantom Christian. God's standards are even higher than that! For us to be acceptable in God's sight, only the righteousness of Christ will do. And that's what every child of God has been given in Christ. "God made him who had no sin to be sin for us, so that in him we might become the righteousness of God" (2 Corinthians 5:21).

If you're truly a Christian, then you're as righteous and acceptable as Jesus Christ is.

When I teach about our acceptance in Christ, I usually ask a series of questions to help drive home the truth that God accepts us for who we are right now.

"How many of you," I ask, "are as righteous and acceptable as I am in the sight of God?"

Believe it or not, most hands go up.

"How many of you are as righteous and acceptable in the sight of God as Billy Graham?" I ask.

Usually about half the audience raise their hands to answer this question.

Next I ask, "How many of you are as righteous and acceptable in the sight of God as the apostle Paul?"

Only about ten percent of the people respond favorably to this question.

Now here's the really tough one: "How many of you are as righteous and acceptable in the sight of God as Jesus Christ?"

Very few hands normally go up.

Why? Because we still think that our acceptance is based upon our performance—on how well we're living up to the standard of the Phantom Christian.

How can I stand up and say that I'm as righteous and acceptable in the sight of God as Jesus Christ?

Because of what I do?

No way! It's because of what He has done. He made me righteous and acceptable in God's sight.

As long as you think that your acceptance is based on your performance, you'll never grow in your Christian life. The truth, however, is that God sees you as totally acceptable right now—

not because of what you do, but because of what Christ has done for you. Romans 15:7 puts it this way: "Accept one another, then, just as Christ accepted you, in order to bring praise to God." If you are in Christ, then through God's grace you are totally acceptable in God's sight.

You no longer have to try to be the Phantom Christian. You are already as righteous as Jesus Christ is. Because of this, it's my prayer that you'll never again wrestle with the question of God's acceptance of you, so that you can now go on to discover the immeasurable wonders of His love.

Chapter 58

Under Construction

Being confident of this, that he who began a good work in you will carry it on to completion until the day of Christ Jesus.

Philippians 1:6

IT'S SO EASY TO JUDGE PEOPLE and say, "I can't believe he did that. I'd never do something like *that*." The Bible warns us about this type of attitude, however. Paul wrote to the Galatians, "Brothers, if someone is caught in a sin, you who are spiritual should restore him gently. But watch yourself, or you also may be tempted" (Galatians 6:1).

All of us are capable of committing *any* sin mentioned in the Bible, given the right circumstances. That's why Paul warns against an attitude of condemnation toward other people.

Because each of us struggles with the desires of the flesh, we need to adopt an attitude of restoration toward other people, realizing that God continues to work in each of our lives. It's like God has put a big sign on the front of each of us which reads "Under Construction."

When you and I come to Christ by faith, we're born again of the Spirit of God, and we become new creatures in Christ. What's new, however, is the spiritual part of us. Neither our bodies nor our souls are born again. We still look the same on the outside, and we're capable of thinking, feeling, and doing the same dumb stuff we did when we were lost.

The difference is that now Christ has come to live inside each of us through the person of the Holy Spirit, and He has left us with the promise "that he who began a good work in you will carry it on to completion until the day of Christ Jesus" (Philippians 1:6).

God isn't finished with any of us yet. He will complete the work He began in us of conforming us to the image of His Son. The apostle John writes, "Dear friends, now we are children of God, and what we will be has not yet been made known. But we know that when he appears, we shall be like him, for we shall see him as he is" (1 John 3:2). When we see Jesus, we will be like Him. This is the hope that we have here and now—not only for ourselves, but for one another.

Even when we struggle with the desires of the flesh, God is at work in our lives. Our struggles don't surprise or frustrate Him. He lives in us, and whether we struggle or not, He continues to conform us to His image. That's what He asks us to trust Him to do—not only in our lives, but also in the lives of others.

We're all in the same boat. If we're to be conformed to the image of Christ, *He* will have to do it. Knowing this is what enables us to do as Paul said—to have an attitude of restoration, not condemnation, toward one another.

There were apple trees all over the area of Indiana where I grew up. We kids used to get those apples when they were still immature—small and hard as rocks—and have fights with them. I had a great feeling of accomplishment when I could really clock one of my buddies in the head with one.

Now were those apples perfect in nature? Yes, absolutely. Everything that would ever be in them was already there. But were they mature? No.

We Christians have been made complete—perfect—in Christ. We are forgiven, redeemed, made spiritually alive, and we stand in the righteousness of Christ, totally accepted.

Are we perfectly mature? No. That won't happen until the day of resurrection, when we receive new bodies to go with the resurrected spirits we already possess.

God has a lot of building and training to do in us yet. We ought to see each other with that invisible sign on our chests reading, "Under Construction." It would make us more tolerant and forgiving toward one another. Until then, we can be sure that God, "who began a good work in you will carry it on to completion until the day of Christ Jesus" (Philippians 1:6).

Even though we're aware of the sometimes difficult process of growth, He sees us as *already there*.

As I said to a radio listener, "God will never love or accept you one ounce less or one ounce more than He does *right this minute*."

That's a truth to build a life on!

Chapter 59

Sharon's Story

ONE NIGHT ON OUR *People to People* broadcast I took a call from a young woman named Sharon.

"I've really benefited from your teaching," she said, "and I'm learning more and more about God's love for me. But I have a situation that I don't know how to handle."

She paused and took a deep breath.

"I'm nineteen years old now, but when I was younger, I was sexually molested by four of my uncles. Since then I've come to know Jesus, and I don't hate them anymore. I've forgiven them.

But the problem is that we have these family reunions where I see all of them, and I don't know how to handle it."

What can you say on live nationwide radio to a question like this? All I know to do is to trust in God and His Word.

"Sharon," I said, "my heart just breaks for you. That's such a terrible thing—it's hard for me to imagine such a background. I'm so thankful that you have come to know Christ, and that He's healing you of the hurt and bitterness that are natural to feel after experiences like yours."

I paused for a moment. "But after all that, Sharon, as much as I may sympathize with you for your past, there's really only one issue that matters right now—because there's nothing you or I or anyone else can do to change the past. The question is, what will you do today and in the future?

"God promised us in Romans 8:28, 'We know that in all things God works for the good of those who love him, who have been called according to his purpose.'

"It doesn't say all things look good, or all things feel good, or even that all things *are* good. It says that God will cause all things to work together for good. I know that's hard to understand, but let's work through it.

"Think about this, Sharon," I continued. "Do you think you'll run into any other women in your life who have been through similar experiences?"

"I'm sure I will," she answered softly, her voice breaking as she tried not to cry.

"I think so, too, Sharon," I said. "How many do you think?"

"I don't know," Sharon responded, "maybe hundreds."

"In this sinful, sad world, that's probably true," I said. "Sharon, the best possible person in the world to minister to those women with the love and compassion of Jesus is somebody who's been there. You see, Sharon, we're called to be servants, just like Christ was. But in order to be an effective servant, we have to have compassion. How do we learn compassion? There's only one way I know of—by going through trials and tribulations ourselves. That's why we read in 2 Corinthians 1:3,4: 'Praise be to the God and Father of our Lord Jesus Christ, the Father of compassion and the God of all comfort, who comforts us in all our troubles, so that we can comfort those in any trouble with the comfort we ourselves have received from God.'

"You see, there's a reason for you to apply the command to 'give thanks in all circumstances' (1 Thessalonians 5:18). Sharon, you can have a thankful heart for a God who loves you and who will take even terrible experiences like yours and turn them into an opportunity for good, as you go free in your own spirit and then reach out and serve others with the same love that you have received from Him."

Sharon immediately perceived the truth of these things. Her peace and freedom of spirit were a vivid illustration of the results of allowing God to renew our minds (Romans 12:2), which I define as looking at ourselves and our circumstances from God's perspective rather than from man's perspective.

And that's exactly what Sharon did. With her circumstances and reactions in proper focus, we moved on to discuss how to deal with her uncles.

"Sharon, you can't pretend that nothing ever happened," I said. "So my advice to you is to deal with it directly. You could approach each one and say, 'We both know what went on in the past. But I want you to know that Jesus Christ is now my Lord. He's forgiven me of my sins, He's provided for the forgiveness of your sins, and I forgive you, too.'

"Do any of your uncles know the Lord?" I asked.

"No," she answered.

I asked if she knew how to share the gospel, and again she said no.

"I'll tell you what I'll do. We've written a little booklet that explains how to come to know Christ, and I'll send you one right away. It's very simple; all you have to do is read it with someone."

Sharon was excited about the idea, and we concluded our phone conversation.

Three days later, Sharon called back.

"Over the weekend," she said, "we had another family gathering, and the booklet you talked about didn't arrive in time. But I did as you suggested. I talked to each of my four uncles personally, and I led two of them to the Lord!"

What a miracle! A poor innocent child, abused in a degrading way, growing into a strong, compassionate, and clearsighted young woman. She had every reason to hang on to self-pity, hatred, and bitterness for a lifetime, and the world would have encouraged her to do so. But instead she became preoccupied with the living Christ and, controlled by His love, she chose to respond to adversity in God's way.

Sharon could have viewed herself as a victim, but she chose instead to view herself as God sees her—a child of God who has already received "everything [she needs] for life and godliness" (2 Peter 1:3).

Sharon experienced a changed life because she experienced an *exchanged* life in Jesus Christ! Now she's free and is helping other people to see and understand their freedom in Christ.

Sharon's life shows the power of the exchanged life. It's not enough to have glib answers to people's problems. Sometimes when we're without compassion, we become like vending machines. A person shares a personal heartache with us, and out pops a Bible verse.

Even biblical truth, such as "give thanks in all circumstances," can be harmful when shared at the wrong time or in the wrong spirit—particularly when it's shared apart from a heart of compassion.

In order to apply biblical principles for living, we must have the biblical foundation of understanding God's love and acceptance. Giving thanks in times of trouble makes no sense to us unless we're seeing our lives and ourselves from God's perspective.

It's also not enough to tell people what they should stop doing. How could Sharon, for example, simply stop feeling the very understandable emotions of bitterness, hatred, and self-pity?

There's only one way: by developing a totally new mind-set, a new preoccupation.

I wish I had the space to tell a hundred more stories like Sharon's of how the message of God's grace powerfully changes lives, but that would take a whole library.

Each such grace story stands as proof that the truth really does set you free. People continue to argue and nit-pick over theological issues but, to use an old phrase, "the proof of the pudding is in the eating."

The power of the undiluted gospel to transform lives is unexplainable by any natural means. If there's a single principle that sums up the life of freedom under grace, to me it's the one expressed in Galatians 5:13: "You were called to freedom, brethren; only do not turn your freedom into an opportunity for the flesh, but through love serve one another" (NASB).

The Lord Jesus said in regard to His own life, "The Son of Man did not come to be served, but to serve, and to give his life as a ransom for many" (Matthew 20:28). He also said, "'It is more blessed to give than to receive'" (Acts 20:35).

Paul added, "Do nothing out of selfish ambition or vain conceit, but in humility consider others better than yourselves" (Philippians 2:3).

The unmistakable sign that "Classic Christianity" is taking hold in a person's heart is when you see the beginnings of the same humble attitude that Christ had: "I am not here to be served, but to serve."

There's nothing less natural to a human being than that kind of attitude. Only the miracle of the gospel can produce it. How else can you explain the attitude and actions of someone like Sharon apart from the intervention of a miracle-working God?

In the same way, the message of God's grace hardens the heart of the proud, and softens the heart of the humble. "God opposes the proud but gives grace to the humble" (James 4:6).

Why is grace only available to the humble?

Because only the humble will receive it. The humble will always find God to be gracious and compassionate. He will open the floodgates of His love to any man, woman, boy, or girl who comes to Him in humble faith.

Every reader of this book has had or can have his or her own "grace story" to tell. God can speak to you through His natural world or through some specially designed circumstances that illustrate His truth in the Bible.

The Lord continues to say to you and to me: "Here I am! I stand at the door and knock. If anyone hears my voice and opens the door, I will come in and eat with him, and he with me" (Revelation 3:20).

Open the door of your heart, and discover that "Classic Christianity" is a Person—the living Lord Jesus Christ.

The Puzzle Comes Together

I HOPE YOU'VE BENEFITED FROM reading the preceding grace stories, and I have one last illustration I'd like to leave you with before you go.

Many Christians' faith can be compared to a big box of jigsaw puzzle pieces, each piece representing a Bible verse, a sermon illustration, or a doctrine they've been taught over the years. If they've been Christians very long at all, they've probably accumulated quite a collection! I know that's how I was for many years. I had collected quite an assortment of good doctrines, sermons, and such. But have you ever tried to put together a jigsaw puzzle without the cover of the box that shows what the finished picture should look like?

You pick up a piece: "Well, it's got a little red, a little green, and a little white in it," you say. "But I don't have a clue to what it is."

So you pick up another piece that also has some red, green, or white. The two pieces don't fit easily, but with a little brute force you can make them stay together. Unfortunately, the union of the two still doesn't look like anything recognizable. That's how I was—stuck with a lot of puzzle pieces without an understanding of how they fitted together. I know from my years of counseling that there are many other Christians who feel the same way.

But when someone finally gives you the cover of the box to compare the pieces to, you can easily identify where each piece goes.

"Now I see," you say. "The red on this piece is part of that barn, the green is part of the tree, and the white is part of the sheet hanging on the line. Oh, here's another part of the barn, and it fits like so."

How much easier it is to identify the small pieces when you can put them into a context! And that's exactly what God did for me, through opening my understanding to the "life and death" issue of salvation.

God took me back to a bird's-eye view of the whole Bible, which immediately caused hundreds of small pieces that we call verses to fall into place. There weren't any new verses. I knew them all well. But finally I could see where they fit without having to apply brute force!

As I've had the pleasure of teaching thousands of people the same life-transforming truths, I've heard them say again and again, "For the first time in my life, I can understand my Bible!" They always say this with a sense of wonder. That shows you that they had, in their hearts, given up any hope of being able to put the jigsaw puzzle pieces of their faith into an arrangement that worked in daily life.

Rooting yourself in God's grace and trusting in it alone enables you to see the whole of Christian faith in all its glory. The puzzle is complete. Every piece makes sense when it's understood in relation to the whole picture.

My hope is that through these grace stories you've had a chance to see the top of the puzzle box. I hope you're beginning to see how all the pieces fit.

It's my prayer that in the weeks and months ahead, you'll start seeing the pieces fit in place as you read the Bible, fellowship with other believers, and enjoy friendship with God based on His wonderful grace.

Also, I hope as God moves in your life, every so often you'll find yourself saying of a certain situation you've experienced, "That's a grace story from God."

People to People
MINISTRIES

Bob George can be heard live
each weekday on *People to People!*

The longest-running live national call-in
biblical counseling program on Christian radio.

Bob George, host
of *People to People*

Live!
Monday - Friday
3:30pm - 4:00pm CST
6:05pm - 7:00pm CST

For a listing of radio stations in your area,
call **1-800-727-2828,** or visit us on the Internet at:
www.realanswers.net

Real Answers
for
Real Life™

Call 1-800-677-9377
to participate in the radio program.